W9-AUD-716

HISTORY OF SPORTS

TRACK AND FIELD

Titles in The History of Sports series include:

TRACK AND FIELD

BY NATHAN AASENG

Lucent Books, Inc.
San Diego, California

Library of Congress Cataloging-in-Publication Data

Aaseng, Nathan.
    Track and field / by Nathan Aaseng.
        p.   cm. — (History of sports)
    Includes bibliographical references and index.
    ISBN 1-56006-960-0 (hard : alk. paper)
    1. Track–athletics—History—Juvenile literature. [1. Track
and field—History. 2. Track and field athletes. 3. Olympics—
History.] I. Title. II. Series.
    GV1060.55 .A38   2002
    796.42—dc21

2001000856

Contents

MORE THAN MANY areas of human endeavor, sports give us the opportunity to see the possibilities in our physical selves. As participants, we all too quickly find limits to how fast we can run, how high we can jump, how far and straight we can hit a golf ball. But as spectators we can surpass those limits as we view the accomplishments of others and see how fast, how smooth, and how strong a human being can be. We marvel at the gravity-defying leaps of a Michael Jordan as he strains towards a basketball hoop or at the dribbling of a Mia Hamm as she eludes defenders on the soccer field. We shake our heads in disbelief at the talents of a young Tiger Woods hitting an approach shot to the green or the speed of a Carl Lewis as he appears to glide around an Olympic track.

These are what the sports media call "the oohs and ahhs" of sports—the stuff of highlight reels and *Sports Illustrated* covers. But to understand a sport only in the context of its most artistic modern athletes is shortsighted, for it does little justice to the accomplishments of the athletes *or* to the sport itself. Far more wise is to view a sport as a continuum—a constantly moving, evolving process. On this continuum are not only the superstars of today, but the people who first played the sport, who thought about rules and strategies that would make it more challenging to play as well as a delight to watch.

Lucent Books' series, *The History of Sports,* provides such a continuum. Each book explores the development of a sport from its basic roots onward, and tries to answer questions that a reader might wonder about. Who were its first players, and what sorts of rules did the sport have then? What kinds of equipment were used in the beginning and what changes have taken place over the years?

Each title in *The History of Sports* also identifies key individuals in the sport's history—people whose leadership or skills have made a difference in the way the sport is played today. Included will be the easily recognized names, the Mia Hamms and the Sammy Sosas, the Wilt Chamberlains and the Wilma Rudolphs. But there are also the names of past greats, people like baseball's King Kelly, soccer's Sir Stanley Matthews, and basketball's Hank Luisetti—who may be less familiar today, but were as synonymous with their sports at one time as the "oohs and ahhs" players of today.

Finally, the series looks at the aspects of a sport that are particularly important in its current point on the continuum. Baseball today is better understood knowing about salary caps and union negotiators. One cannot truly know modern soccer without knowing about the specter of fan violence at matches. And learning about the role of instant replay is critical to a thorough understanding of today's professional football games. In viewing a sport as a continuum, the strides that have been made along the way are that much more admirable. It is a richer view, and one that shows how yesterday's limits have been surpassed—and how the limits of today are the possibilities of athletes in the future.

The Purest of Sport

Track and field is the back-to-nature version of sport. The events are simple, the rules few. The contests are so much a part of everyday life that small children participate in them long before they ever hear of, or see an actual competition. From the time they first learn to totter on two legs, children understand the joy of the race—of getting to a destination as fast as their wobbly legs can carry them. Without ever being aware of the Olympic giants who hurl the shot, children delight in the challenge of seeing who can throw a stone the furthest into a glassy pond. In their exuberance, children leap as high into the air as they can, testing the limits of their freedom over the pull of gravity.

Unlike sports such as football and hockey that require a great deal of expensive equip-ment, or sports such as tennis and golf in which access to expensive facilities is a huge advantage, track and field is open to anyone. As Bob Schul, the 1964 Olympic 5,000 meter champion from the United States, said, "You don't have to have good equipment or expensive tracks to train on, and it doesn't matter whether or not you're the poorest nation or person in the world."[1] Track and field has crowned international champions who could not afford shoes to run in.

Track and field has universal appeal be-cause it is athletic competition boiled down to its purest form. In fact, for much of its history, the sport was called, simply, athletics. And virtually every other sport requires one or more of the four athletic skills that track and field tests: speed, strength, agility, and stamina.

The speed displayed by track sprinters is an essential ingredient in many of the most popular sports. It allows football players to outrun opponents to the end zone, tennis players to race across the court to reach a well-placed shot, soccer players to gain control of a loose ball, and baseball players to steal bases. Strength in track and field is demonstrated primarily in throwing objects for distance. Success in baseball depends in large part on this same ability, to hurl an object with considerable force, and the best quarterbacks can throw a football far beyond the efforts of most mortals. The agility shown by track and field's jumpers, vaulters, and hurdlers is the same type of athletic skill

Jackie Joyner-Kersee soars into the air during the women's long jump competition at the 1996 Olympics in Atlanta, Georgia.

that basketball players use to perform twisting reverse layups and soaring slam dunks. In any competition that requires physical exertion, stamina comes in to play, whether it is a hockey player trying to keep going full tilt at the end of a long shift on the ice, or a tennis player trying to keep her focus after playing all day in stifling heat.

Track and field is no longer, at least in the United States, a spectator sport on the level of the other major sports. It is not a team sport, where the fans' stake in rooting for the home team or an adopted favorite keeps them intensely engrossed in every facet of the game. Track and field is such a simple and basic sport that promoters have had great difficulty trying to package it as mass entertainment. Fans who are used to settling in for one continuous three-hour football game do not get the same result when watching a track and field meet where different events are taking place at the same time, and where one race, the 100-meter dash, lasts only about ten seconds.

Furthermore, despite its simplicity, track and field competition has been clouded by the intricacies of modern culture. Because it is an international sport and the showcase of the Olympics, track and field has found itself entangled in a web of political maneuvering. As the incentives of fame and fortune have increased in the modern age, competitors have been tempted to bend or break rules, resulting in an increasing use of technology to police a sport that once required little supervision.

Nonetheless, spectators continue to be intrigued by the efforts of athletes striving to reach the limits of human excellence in speed, strength, agility, and stamina. Athletes continue to be drawn to the challenge of matching their prowess in those categories against others, just as they were drawn to such challenges as small children. And every four years, when the Olympics return to the international scene, track and field resumes its place as the showcase event of the competition. For as long as humans have existed and will exist, there will always remain the urge to see who can earn the undisputed titles as the World's Fastest Human, the World's Greatest Athlete, and other honors bestowed upon the world's track and field champions.

CHAPTER 1

The Olympics: Birth and Rebirth of Track and Field

Footraces have been going on for as long as humans have roamed the earth, and even longer if races between predators and prey animals are counted. The earliest records of organized races for sheer competitive sport date back to Greece in the thirteenth century B.C.

The ancient Greeks' respect for foot speed as an important military asset can be seen in the writings of the poet Homer, in his accounts of the warrior Achilles' swiftness and the contests of speed between the Greek heroes. In 776 B.C., the Greeks established a formal celebration of running talent by organizing a competition held in the city of Olympia. These Olympic Games were considered important enough that wars ceased during the time of the competition.

The first Olympic Games appear to have had only one event, the stade, which was a race the length of the stadium (about 200 meters). A cook named Coroebus was the first recorded winner of this event. Two other events were soon added: the diaculos (a race the length of the stadium and back) and the dolichos (a race that modern scholars estimate to have been about 5 kilometers). As the years went by, throwing events such as the discus and javelin were added. The Greeks were not very interested in jumps, however. Their Olympics offered only the long jump, and even that was included only as part of a multiskill event that also included running and throwing.

In the earlier centuries, the Olympic Games were limited to Greeks only. When the Romans conquered the Greeks, however, they began entering as well and then took over the games. Eventually, the Olympics degenerated into a cheap spectacle for the amusement of the masses. About 392 A.D., the Roman emperor Theodosius branded the games a public nuisance and ordered them terminated. By his one decree, more than 1,100 years worth of track and field tradition was wiped out.

The Nineteenth Century—Emerging from Dormancy

Although it is inconceivable to believe that some sort of informal running and throwing contests did not take place during the cen-

turies that followed, there is no evidence of any organized competitions for nearly a thousand years. In fact, according to Ralph Hickock's *New Encyclopedia of Sports*, "The concept of having a number of track and field events held at the same time, in the same place, apparently dates from twelfth century England."[2] There is evidence that England set aside public areas as early as 1154 for people to practice running, jumping, and throwing. Actual competitions, however, remained an informal, localized affair for centuries.

During the 1820s, track and field as an organized sport was revived along two separate pathways. The first was amateur competition,

The first foot races began in Greece during the thirteenth century B.C.

beginning with the Scottish Border Games, in which local athletes competed simply for the fun or challenge of it, the greatest prizes being ribbons or trophies. This competition spread throughout schools in England until it became one of the nation's most popular sporting events. The organizers of these competitions did not introduce any new events, or make any particular innovations. Tom Mc-Nab, author of *The Complete Book of Track and Field*, says, "The public schools of the mid–nineteenth century . . . simply selected events from the existing rural sport culture."[3]

Meanwhile, in the United States, a group of New Jersey promoters introduced the concept of professional track and field when they put up prize money for a footrace to be held on July 5, 1824. The race attracted little interest, but it did establish a precedent for future contests between champions from different localities. Before long, there were even spirited competitions between the best runners from England and the United States. Interest in professional racing reached its peak in 1849 with the highly publicized long distance races pitting the American Indian, Deerfoot (also known as Louis Bennett) against the cream of British distance runners.

In the years that followed, interest in prize races evaporated. But the growing enthusiasm for contests of speed, strength, agility, and stamina was easily transferred to the school competitions and to amateur athletic clubs. In 1864, England's Oxford and Cambridge Universities met in the first formal collegiate track and field competition. Interest in such competitions spread to the United States where colleges, primarily in New England, began organizing track and field meets. Harvard and Yale particularly dominated the competition among U.S. colleges. Following the formation of the InterCollegiate Athletic Association (ICAA) in the latter nineteenth century, Harvard won eleven ICAA titles and Yale six.

At the same time, amateur running clubs became popular in the United States. In 1868, the New York Athletic Club organized the United States' first track meet, held on an indoor track. The number of amateur running clubs in the country expanded remarkably during the next two decades. According to nineteenth century historian John Cumming, "It was estimated that there were more than 90 athletic clubs in the Eastern seaboard area in 1880."[4] Track meets grew so popular that when the fledgling Amateur Athletic Union (AAU) held an indoor meet in New York City in 1889, more than 1,500 interested spectators were turned away for lack of room.

Interregional rivalries grew up in the United States during the last decades of the eighteenth century. Easterners accused their counterparts in the west of reporting false times and cheating on distances in order to claim world records. A number of Western athletes then traveled east at their own expense to prove their prowess against Easterners. Equally intense was the rivalry between

American and British champion athletes, with both sides claiming superiority. The long-standing debate eventually led to the organization of a full-scale meet between champions of the two nations. This competition, held in 1895 at Travers Island in New York, was the first international track and field meet.

Olympic Revival

At almost the same time, a French nobleman was laying the groundwork for an international competition on a far greater scale, one that would change the nature of track and field forever. In 1887, Baron Pierre de Coubertin observed English college students participating in sports: This led him to think about the importance of physical activity in society. Two years later, he founded the Congress of Physical Education in Paris as a means of promoting sports in French schools.

During his studies on the role of sports in society, de Coubertin was especially intrigued by the concept of the Olympic Games. When the recent success by German archaeologists in uncovering the ruins of ancient Olympia came to his attention, he viewed the ancient Greek games as an ideal way to celebrate the importance of exercise in the education of youth.

In de Coubertin's view, winning was not the primary objective of an Olympic athlete. "The importance of life," he wrote, "is not so much in triumph or winning as in the struggle itself; the prime essential is not so much to have conquered as to have performed honorably and well."[5] Professional athletes, who competed for the sole purpose of winning and thereby making a profit from their efforts, had no place in such a philosophy.

During a lecture in 1892, de Coubertin first proposed reviving a form of the ancient Olympic Games. But while the competition would be based on the Greek format, he proposed opening it to athletes throughout the world. De Coubertin invited interested persons (all of whom were solidly upper class) to

Frenchman Baron Pierre de Coubertin, founder of the modern Olympic Games.

join him in forming the modern Olympics. At an organizational meeting in 1894, this group decided to honor the tradition of the Greeks by holding the first competition in Athens, Greece. A wealthy Greek named George Averoff donated a huge sum of money to construct the needed stadium.

On April 6, 1896, 285 athletes from thirteen nations gathered in Athens to rekindle the Olympic competition. Although a spattering of other sports such as swimming and target shooting were included, the main emphasis of the competition was track and field. More than 100,000 spectators crammed in the stadium to watch the athletes, and many

thousands more viewed the action from the hills overlooking the stadium.

The most dramatic moment of those first modern Olympics came in an event specially created for this competition from an ancient Greek legend. Olympic organizers had decided to conclude the program with an exhausting race from the town of Marathon to the stadium at Athens, a distance of about twenty-five miles. This was to commemorate the heroic efforts of Pheidippides, a Greek messenger, who ran the distance in 490 B.C. to announce the news of the Greeks' defeat of the Persian army and then died of exhaustion on the spot.

The 1896 Olympics in Athens, Greece, featured 285 athletes from thirteen nations and welcomed more than 100,000 spectators.

U.S. INVOLVEMENT IN THE FIRST OLYMPICS

Most of the participants in the first modern Olympics came from European nations. The exception was a team of athletes, including ten track and field participants, from the United States. Since the Olympics were conceived as strictly a competition between individuals, none of the athletes received any government support. Therefore, the Americans' willingness to travel across the ocean by boat to take part in the games required an enormous commitment of time and money. College freshman James B. Connolly had to make an even greater sacrifice when Harvard University denied his request for a leave of absence to participate in the Olympics. Connolly dropped out of school, never to return, in order to make the trip. The most enthusiastic U.S. supporter of the modern Olympics was Robert Garrett, a track captain at Princeton University. Garrett not only paid his own way to Athens, but picked up the tab so that three of his Princeton teammates could also compete in the games.

The long voyage turned out to be well worth the effort for the U.S. team. Connolly won the first gold medal of the modern Olympics by winning the triple jump. Garrett pulled off the incredible feat of winning an event that he entered at the last minute on a lark. Working from pictures of the ancient Greek discus, Garrett had tried to make one back at Princeton, but without success. Upon arriving at Athens, and seeing an actual discus, he could not resist the impulse to try the event. Although fearful of making a fool of himself, Garrett stunned the spectators by defeating the Greek champion to win the gold medal. Garrett also claimed first place in the shot put. Altogether, the team that traveled the farthest for the games walked off with gold medals in nine of the twelve track and field events.

The crowds packing the stadium waited anxiously for the arrival of the winner. Many of them were desperately hoping that one of their own citizens could salvage the honor of Greece, which had not won any of the other events. A roar of celebration erupted when Spiridon Louis, a Greek shepherd, arrived at the stadium in first place—leaving the Olympic organizers basking in a glow of good will.

The Olympic Games Stumble

Having succeeded beyond their expectations with the Athens Games, de Coubertin and his associates believed they had laid the foundation for a permanent Olympics. They scheduled the next competition for 1900, following the Greek tradition of an Olympic contest every four years.

In selecting the site of the second Olympics, however, organizers made a major blunder. Hoping to take advantage of the publicity generated by the 1900 Universal Exposition being held in Paris, Olympic officials arranged to have their competition included as part of that celebration. But instead of benefiting from interest in the exposition, the Olympics got lost in it. The French officials in charge of the games were so careless in their organization that

The 1900 U.S. Olympic team. That year, the Games were overshadowed by the Paris Universal Exposition.

they did not even bother to build a cinder track, the standard surface for running races. To the astonishment of the participants, the events had to be held on grass. The name "Olympics" was not even on the track and field program, and even some of the winners were unaware, until they received their medals, that the track meet had anything to do with a larger event called the Olympics. According to Lewis H. Carlson and John J. Fogarty, in *Tales of Gold*, "The 1900 Paris Games were so poorly run that nobody took them very seriously, including Baron de Coubertin."[6]

The same mistake occurred in 1904, when the Olympics were initially awarded to Chicago, only to have St. Louis use some political muscle to claim them as part of that year's gigantic Louisiana Purchase Exposition. Much of the competition in St. Louis more closely resembled a carnival attraction than a serious sporting event. The problem was compounded by the remoteness of St. Louis from the countries that had participated in previous Olympics. Many athletes were either unwilling or unable to make the journey. Neither France nor England sent any athletes, and foreign competition was so scarce that observers remarked that they could just as well be watching a meet between track clubs from New York and Chicago.

There was some question whether the spirit of the 1896 Games could be revived after two such fiascos. Fortunately, the Greeks put on their own competition in 1906 to celebrate the ten-year anniversary of those first modern games. While not an official Olympics in the eyes of many officials, this return to a well-run, no-nonsense track meet helped reestablish the principles that de Coubertin and others had been trying to establish.

The 1908 Olympics, however, brought more confusion and controversy. Originally slated for Rome, they had to be moved to London when the Italians backed out. Although far better organized than previous

NEVER ON SUNDAY

During the early years of the Olympics and international track and field competition, one of the most furious controversies concerned competing on Sundays. At that time a number of mainstream religious denominations, particularly in the United States and Great Britain, taught that God intended Sunday, the Sabbath, to be a day of rest. Some followers of these faiths were more strict than others in their interpretation of this rule. For some, it meant no work of any kind, including cooking meals; for others, it simply meant not working at a job or any other strenuous tasks. A sizable number of athletes also believed that the Sabbath day of rest prohibited participation in competitive sporting events. Out of respect for this belief, few sporting events were held on Sunday in the United States.

Such a belief was not common in France, however, and organizers of the 1900 Paris Olympics showed no sympathy with those who followed it. Thus, a number of track and field events were scheduled for a Sunday. Following protests from the United States and others, French officials wavered, but then held fast to their schedule. Eight of the fifteen U.S. track and field athletes refused to compete on Sunday. Athletes from the University of Pennsylvania did compete, however, winning several gold medals and greatly angering their American teammates in the process.

Twenty years later, Sunday competition was still a hot issue, with the French again serving as hosts. Scottish sprinter Eric Liddell, whose career was later chronicled in the popular movie *Chariots of Fire,* learned that the finals of his best event, the 100-meter dash, were to be held on a Sunday. A devout son of a missionary, Liddell would not compete on Sunday so he passed up the 100 in favor of the 200- and 400-meter races. Liddell took considerable criticism from fans in his home country for being "unpatriotic" in passing up a chance to add to his country's medal total. But the affair ended happily for him. Although he was not highly ranked at 400 meters, he shocked both competitors and supporters by winning the event in 47.6 seconds, smashing the old Olympic mark by two full seconds.

Since the 1950s, religious opposition to sporting contests on Sunday has diminished greatly. In fact, Sunday is now one of the prime days for athletic competition, and athletes who express concerns or avoid Sunday competition are rare.

At the 1908 London Olympics, British runner Wyndham Halswelle (second from left) won the gold medal after re-running the race alone.

efforts, these Games were marred by constant bickering between participants and the British track and field judges. The worst example was the 400-meter run, in which U.S. runner John Carpenter ran wide down the finishing stretch, tangling with British runner Wyndham Halswelle, who was trying to pass him. British officials broke the finishing tape before the runners arrived, disqualified Carpenter, and ordered the race rerun. Arguments between supporters of Halswelle and Carpenter grew so heated that it was a half hour be-fore officials could clear them off the track. The rerun turned out to be a farce when the rest of the competitors refused to participate. Halswelle had to run by himself and sheepishly accepted a very unsatisfying gold medal. He was so disgusted with the whole matter that he never ran competitively again.

Solid Footing for Track and Field

The Olympics seemed to be accomplishing just the opposite of what had been intended:

Instead of promoting international cooperation, they were fostering ill will. More calls arose for the Games to be disbanded. However, just as de Coubertin's vision seemed destined to fade into oblivion, the Swedes rescued the Olympics in 1912, with a superbly well-administered and fair competition. These games included athletes from twenty-six different nations, and the performances were so inspiring that the Olympics became front page news across much of the world.

Capitalizing on the success of the Stockholm Games, track and field enthusiasts organized the International Amateur Athletic Federation (IAAF) in 1913 to set standards and oversee the development of international track and field competition. The strong framework established by the 1912 Olympics and the IAAF allowed the sport to survive the grim interruption of World War I. At the war's conclusion, international track and field and Olympic competition resumed without missing a beat.

Growth of Track and Field

During these formative years of international track and field competition, the events were almost exclusively a test of raw talent and work ethic. Athletes trained and competed on their own, using whatever techniques or strategies they could create. Bud Houser, who won Olympic gold medals in both the shot put and the discus in 1924, described the haphazard nature of his sport:

"There really weren't any coaches around for field sports. Boy, we didn't know what we were doing. We just had to try to work things out for ourselves."[7]

THE ST. LOUIS CIRCUS

If the shabby organization of the 1900 Paris Games undermined the prestige of the Olympics, the bizarre character of the 1904 Games in St. Louis nearly finished it off for good. Although the Olympic name was used to promote it, the sports program included a lengthy list of often strange and tasteless events spread over a period of four and a half months. Among the track and field events, for example, was a track meet for thirteen-year olds. The part of the program that embarrassed Olympic officials the most was a shameful exhibition of racism trumpeted as "Anthropology Days," in which, according to Bill Henry, in *An Approved History of the Olympics,* "a collection of aboriginal freaks, rumored to have been drafted from the sideshows of the exposition, went through the motions of athletic competition, to the vast amusement of a handful of spectators." De Coubertin could only shake his head in disbelief and, according to Allen Guttman, in *The Olympics,* mutter, "In no place but America would one have dared place such events on a program."

The St. Louis Games even managed to make a mess of the prestigious marathon. At the end of the race, Fred Lorz of New York arrived in the stadium, amazingly fresh, to claim victory over Thomas Hicks of Massachusetts. The reason for his lack of fatigue, however, was quickly uncovered. Lorz had hitched a ride on a truck over several miles of the course before jumping out near the stadium to claim victory.

Finnish discus-thrower Armas Taipale, gold medal winner at the 1912 Stockholm Games. Finland was the first nation to demonstrate the effectiveness of an organized training program for athletes.

With every athlete having to resort to trial and error, performances in track and field improved slowly. McNab noted that, even by 1930, "From a technical point of view, athletics had advanced little since the nineteenth century."[8]

It was the Finns who started the trend toward more thorough and systematic training in track and field. Finland was the first nation to support the training of a large team of athletes for international competition. This effort paid off handsomely beginning in 1912, as the tiny country won three gold medals and finished second to the United States in total medals. Having demonstrated the value of an organized training program, the Finns continued with it and produced even more astounding results in the 1920s. During the 1920 Olympics, Finnish athletes won the 10,000 meter run, marathon, shot put, triple jump, discus, and javelin. Finland's highly trained distance runners became so dominant that they won gold medals in every distance event in the 1924 Olympics: the 1,500 meters, 5,000 meters, 10,000 meters, marathon, and 3,000 meter steeplechase.

Following the disruption of track and field in the late 1930s and 1940s due to World War II, innovative coaches, government-sponsored programs, and increased international interest ushered in a new era of track and field. Until shortly after the end of World War II, track and field had been primarily a European and American phenomenon. In the 1950s, though, the Soviet Union joined international track and field competition. The lesson of the Finns was not lost on the Soviets, and they burst onto the scene with a stable of talented, highly coached, and well-subsidized athletes. In the 1970s, East Germany placed an even more intense national emphasis on sports and vaulted their nation to the top of international competition.

At the same time that increased training and sports research efforts were changing the track and field world, international interest in the sport was soaring. The sport received perhaps its greatest boost in 1960 when the

Rome Olympics were televised. For the first time, young athletes around the world had a chance to see the greatest track and field stars in action. Many of these young observers set their sights on attaining their own gold medal someday. As a result, international track and field spread to include athletes from Third World nations. Some of these nations, particularly Kenya, began tapping into the huge potential of their distance runners.

High-Stakes Venture

As the showcase event of track and field, the Olympics grew steadily in stature and in participation until it became a multibillion dollar business. Television advertisers invested billions of dollars in advertising at the Games, as did companies seeking endorsements from star athletes. By the 1990s, as rules restricting the Olympics to amateur athletes fell by the wayside, this money began flowing more freely to the athletes themselves.

This meant that by the turn of the twenty-first century, international track and field had become a high-stakes venture. The rewards of a successful track and field career grew so great that top stars such as Carl Lewis and Michael Johnson were able to become wealthy individuals. The lure of huge rewards has made competition today so fierce that world-class athletes must take advantage of every advance in physiology, kinesiology, psychology, and nutrition to keep pace with their rivals.

CHAPTER 2

Evolution of Track and Field

E ven in as basic a sport as track and field, standards and procedures have changed over time. Over the course of two centuries, track and field events have evolved from fairly informal contests whose rules were largely determined by the host team, to highly structured, tightly regulated competitions. In addition, advances in technology have influenced the nature of today's track and field meets.

Standardization of Distances

Beginning with the first national championships in 1876, U.S. track organizations measured their racing distances in yards, a practice that continued for nearly a century. These distances were similar to the metric distances used by the rest of the world: the 100-yard dash is slightly shorter than the 100-meter dash and the mile is roughly 100 meters longer than the 1,500 meter race. All Olympic and international competitions, however, used metric distances.

After 1973, American athletes joined the rest of the world and switched to metric distances for all meets, thus eliminating the need for two separate sets of world records. Although distances in the field events are recorded in metric measurements, results are converted to feet and inches in the United States for the benefit of a public less familiar with metric distances.

Standardization of Surfaces

Beginning in the nineteenth century, British and U.S. track and field officials decided to provide a uniform surface on which track events would be run. They chose crushed cinder or clay tracks because this type of material could be rolled to a smooth, even surface. Rather than wearing out like grass, it could be rerolled when torn up by runners. There was one major drawback, however; these tracks deteriorated terribly in rain.

During both London Olympics in 1908 and in 1948, and again in the 1964 Games in Tokyo, competitors had to slog through mud and even standing water during their events.

These problems led to the development of rubberized synthetic tracks and runways that were waterproof and offered a solid, yet springy surface for competitors. The

Spattered with mud, runners compete on a rain-soaked track during the 1948 Olympics. Such conditions led to the development of waterproof synthetic tracks and runways.

Numerous false starts during Olympic races prompted officials to institute a rule that sprinters be allowed only one false start before being disqualified.

synthetic track made its Olympic debut in the 1968 Olympics in Mexico City. These tracks proved to be so superior that all major international track and field competitions since then have used them. Now, even the majority of high school track teams in the United States operate on synthetic surfaces.

The Start

The problem of ensuring a fair start proved more difficult than providing a fair and uniform running surface. Sprinters in the early years made an art out of beating the starting gun or timing their start so that they were running just as the gun went off. Near the turn of the twentieth century, one track competitor complained that "starting methods so loose as to almost permit flyers [running starts]"[9] made it impossible to fairly compare times of various runners.

In the early competitions, officials could stop a race and order it rerun whenever a competitor started early. But there was no penalty for starting early or "false starting," so sprinters kept trying to beat the start. Such tactics made a farce of the 100-meter dash in the 1912 Olympics. The U.S.' top sprinter, Ralph Craig, false started three times in the finals that year, and his competitors contributed four more false starts. On the eighth attempt, the sprinters finally got away cleanly, and Craig won the race. To prevent repeat occurrences of such a fiasco, track and field officials eventually limited sprinters to one false start each. Upon a second false start, the competitor was disqualified from the race.

Yet even this did not ease the difficulty of determining whether a sprinter moved a blink of an eye before the gun. In the 1990s, technology came to the rescue. Starting blocks at all Olympic short distance events are now equipped with pressure pads, wired to the starting gun, that can detect whether a movement occurred before the starting signal.

Starting blocks also came into use only after a long process of trial and error. European runners during the eighteenth century simply stood poised at the starting line, waiting for the starting signal. American runners, however, found they could get a faster start from a deep crouch than from a standing start. Using this technique, the Americans won virtually every sprinting gold medal in the 1896 Olympics. This prompted the rest of the world to adopt the style.

Crouches became deeper and deeper, and sprinters also took on the technique of pushing hard off the ground to launch themselves into their sprint. Until World War II, sprinters used hand trowels to dig a small hole against which their feet could push. Beginning in the late 1930s, this was replaced by

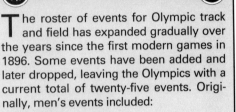

OLYMPIC TRACK AND FIELD EVENTS

The roster of events for Olympic track and field has expanded gradually over the years since the first modern games in 1896. Some events have been added and later dropped, leaving the Olympics with a current total of twenty-five events. Originally, men's events included:

100 meters
400 meters
800 meters
1,500 meters
marathon
110-meter high hurdles
pole vault
long jump
high jump
triple jump
shot put
discus

Currently both men and women participate in:

100 meters
200 meters
400 meters
800 meters
1,500 meters
5,000 meters
10,000 meters
4 x 100 meter relay
4 x 400 meter relay
marathon
110-meter hurdles (100 meters for women)
400-meter hurdles
3,000 meter steeplechase (men only)
20-kilometer walk
50-kilometer walk (men only)
long jump
high jump
triple jump
pole vault
discus
javelin
shot put
hammer throw
decathlon (men only)
heptathlon (women only)

starting blocks which were anchored to the ground and featured adjustable pads to provide support for the feet.

At first, track officials considered blocks to be an artificial advantage and refused to recognize any times set using them as world records. But because starting blocks were a simple device that could provide a uniformly smooth start for all competitors, this stance was soon rescinded. By the 1950s starting blocks became standard equipment for most sprinters. Not all sprinters used them, however, until 1980 when the International Amateur Athletic Federation required their use in international competition for all races up to 400 meters.

Timing

The timing of racers was an even more haphazard feature of early sprint events than the starts themselves. Timers used stopwatches, starting their devices at the crack of the gun and stopping them when the runner crossed the tape. This process, however, relied on fallible human reflexes and judgment. Officials reacted with different speeds to the report of the starting gun and to the blurred image of sprinters flashing across a finish line. The human factor further muddled world records because of what one early track and field expert described as an "overweening desire of timers to attest to a remarkable sprinting performance."[10]

Michael Johnson celebrates next to a scoreboard displaying his new world record time in the 400 meters. Electronic timing devices can record times to the nearest hundredth of a second.

The differences in reaction times were only a minor concern in the eighteenth century when stopwatches could only record times to the nearest one-fifth of a second. When stopwatch accuracy increased to the nearest one-tenth of a second at the 1912 Olympics, there was more cause for concern. Still, reasonable accuracy could be assured by requiring three separate stopwatches to verify a world record time.

However, as electronic timing devices were designed to be capable of distinguishing between the nearest hundredth of a second, the human factor became more limiting. In the 1970s, timing devices in major competitions became completely automatic—linked electronically to a starting gun and to the finish line.

The Finish

Not only were early track officials frustrated by difficulties in ensuring accurate timing, but they occasionally had problems simply determining in what order the contestants finished. In many races, the competitors were so evenly matched that several appeared to cross the finish line at the same time. The solution to this problem was photography, which could stop the action and record it. In 1912, officials began experimenting with a camera positioned at the finish line that would capture the positions of the racers at the exact moment that the first one crossed the finish line.

The techniques of the photo finish were gradually refined so that by the 1932 Olympics, they could dramatically demonstrate their value. In the men's 100-meter dash, Eddie Tolan of the United States started fast, only to be caught by teammate Ralph Metcalfe at 80 meters. Metcalfe inched ahead from there, only to be caught at the finish by a furious last surge from Tolan. The Americans appeared to have hit the finish line at exactly the same time.

Had a photograph of the finish not been available, the judges would not have known for certain who won the race, or if it were actually a tie. But several hours after the race, seven judges sat down to review the film. From this, they were able to determine that Metcalfe had leaned into the finish line just ahead of Tolan. However, Metcalfe had coasted into the tape while Tolan was still accelerating, so Tolan's body crossed the line perhaps two inches ahead of Metcalfe.

This brought up a second controversial issue, the matter of exactly when the race ended. Was it over when the winner's foot crossed the finish line, or could a sprinter lean and get his head across the line to win, or did the entire body have to get across? In the early days of Olympic sprinting, the rule stated that the first person to get his or her torso across the line was the winner. According to those rules, Tolan was awarded the gold. The 1932 race produced so much argument, though, that the rule was subsequently changed so that the winner now is the first person to have any part of his or her torso reach the finish line.

A KING'S WHIM

Dorando Pietri never won a major international race, but he provided track and field fans with perhaps the most dramatic finish in the history of the sport. The intense and bitter rivalry between the U.S. and British teams had reached a fever pitch prior to the marathon at the 1908 Olympics. Fans of both nations desperately wanted their man to win. Yet the first runner to reach the stadium was Pietri, a tiny Italian candymaker. Dressed in red trousers cut off at the knee and a white shirt, he staggered into the packed stadium, stopped completely, and then started the wrong way around the track for the final lap. Officials quickly steered him in the right direction, but it was obvious that something was seriously wrong with the runner. In the words of one reporter, quoted in *Track & Field: The New York Times Encyclopedia of Sports*, "Staggering like a drunken man, he slowly tottered down the homestretch. Three times he fell, and each time, aided by track officials, he fought his way toward the tape."

The drama was compounded when the second-place runner, Johnny Hayes of the United States, entered the stadium. The last thing the British crowd wanted to see was an American victory, yet Pietri was utterly exhausted. As the Italian stumbled around the track, fans grew increasingly frantic. Pietri was barely conscious. Olympic physicians poured stimulants down his throat, hoping to revive him. But as a comparatively fresh Hayes toured the track, it appeared that Pietri, only yards from the finish line after more than three hours of running, would not finish the race. In a rush of desperation, British officials pushed, dragged, and carried the comatose Italian across the finish line, to roars of approval from the crowd.

Compassionate as their gesture may have been, it was for nought. The rules stated that a runner must complete the race under his

Track officials help Dorando Pietri across the finish line during the 1908 Olympic marathon.

own power, and Olympic officials had no choice but to disqualify Pietri.

Ironically, Pietri would have won his gold medal were it not for a whim of the king of England. The original distance of the marathon was 25 miles, the distance between the Greek cities of Marathon and Athens. But in order to allow his grandchildren to see the event, the king requested that the start be moved to the lawn in front of Windsor Castle. It was too late to redraw the race route, so the race was simply lengthened to include the distance from the original start to the castle. This made the 1908 marathon 26 miles, 385 yards. Had it remained the original distance, Pietri would have won easily.

Track and field officials apparently had far more respect for the English king than for Greek tradition. Following the 1908 Olympics, the marathon distance was standardized at the new 26 miles, 385 yards, and has remained so ever since.

The closest race in Olympic history took place in the 1992 women's 100-meter dash. Even with a photograph, judges debated long over the order of finish in a race in which the top five runners were separated by an almost indiscernible .06 seconds.

Event Rules: The Sprints

The first modern Olympics included only twelve track and field events. Over the years a number of events have been added, altered, and discontinued. Although each of the original twelve events remains, all have been altered and expanded somewhat by technology, rule changes, and advances in technique and training.

The 1896 Olympics included two sprints: the 100 meters and the 400 meters. The 220-yard dash had been a staple of U.S. competition since the early days of organized competition, and its metric equivalent was added to the Olympics in 1900. In 1908, the 4 x 400 meter relay made its way onto the event roster, followed four years later by the 4 x 100 meter relay. Both relays required 20-meter zones in which baton exchanges from one runner to another must be completed.

In the 1992 women's 100-meter dash, the top five runners were separated by only .06 seconds, making it the closest race in Olympic history.

From the beginning of Olympic competition, competitors ran the entire race, both the 100-meter and 200-meter dash, in lanes (eventually standardized at 1.2 meters in width) to keep them from interfering with other runners. That posed a problem in running the 200-meter dash, because the further a lane is from the inside of the curve, the further the distance the competitor must run to reach the finish line. As a result, a staggered start had to be used: The starting line for each lane was measured at 200 meters from the finish. The relays also required the use of staggered starts and staggered exchange zones.

Unlike the shorter sprints, the 400 meters was initially run without lanes, which allowed competitors to maneuver for inside position once the starting gun sounded. But the jostling in the 1908 finals between Hal-swelle of Great Britain and Carpenter of the United States was followed in 1912 by another bumping incident during a preliminary round that produced yet another disqualification controversy. As a result, the host Swedes decided to avoid further problems by running the rest of the 400-meter races in lanes, a practice that has been followed ever since.

Event Rules: Hurdles

Hurdle races were an important feature of nineteenth century English track and field, and a 120-yard hurdle race was included in the first U.S. AAU track championships in 1876. In 1896, Olympic officials initiated the 110-meter high hurdles, the metric equivalent of the traditional U.S. hurdle distance, with ten hurdles standing at the height of 3 feet, 6 inches. The event has remained unchanged to

Until the 1930s, hurdlers were disqualified for hitting three or more hurdles during a race.

this day, except for the consequences of hitting hurdles. Athletes used to be disqualified for hitting three or more hurdles during a race. This happened to George Guthrie of the United States who crossed the finish line first in the 110-meter hurdles at the 1924 Olympics. However, during the 1930s, after U.S. track coach Harry Hillman invented weighted L-shaped hurdles that did not fly into other lanes when hit, track organizations lifted the disqualification rule for hitting hurdles, as well as the requirement that a hurdler must cleanly clear all hurdles in order for his time to count as a world record.

Long hurdle races evolved gradually during the early twentieth century. In 1900, the Paris Olympics introduced the 400-meter hurdles, using 30-foot long telephone poles as obstacles, and adding a water jump before the finish line. The water was eliminated in subsequent years, and the hurdles standardized at a height of 3 feet.

Event Rules: Distance Running

Because distance running is perhaps the most basic contest in the world of sports, rule changes and controversies have been few and far between. The only rule change of any consequence over the years has to do with the setting of world records. In distance running, leading a race requires a greater expenditure of both physical and mental energy than following. Therefore, fast times are easier to record if the world's top runners

THE WORLD'S GREATEST ATHLETES

After United States athletes totally dominated track and field events in the early Olympics, some Europeans complained it was because Americans were specialists while Europe produced better all-around athletes. Partly for this reason, the 1912 Olympics in Stockholm, Sweden, added two multiple-skills contests: the pentathlon and the decathlon. The pentathlon consisted of the long jump, javelin, 200 meters, discus, and 1,500 meters, while the decathlon was comprised of the 100-meter, 400-meter, and 1,500-meter runs, the 110-meter hurdles, shot put, javelin, discus, high jump, long jump, and pole vault. A complex scoring system was devised, awarding points to athletes in each event based on how close they came to the existing world record.

Ironically, it was an American, Jim Thorpe, who captured both the pentathlon and the decathlon in the 1912 Olympics. His performance moved the king of Sweden to declare Thorpe the World's Greatest Athlete. That title has been bestowed upon the Olympic decathlon winner ever since.

The men's pentathlon was abandoned after 1924. The decathlon, meanwhile, has undergone periodic revisions in the scoring tables, but has retained the same ten events.

can follow the lead of another fast runner for part, or most of the race.

In the early part of the century, track officials considered it unsporting for distance runners to use a "rabbit," a person who enters a race for the sole purpose of setting a strong early pace for other runners. After

Introduced at the 1920 Olympics, the steeplechase combines running and jumping over obstacles, including 3-foot high hurdles and a 12-foot long water pit.

setting their swift pace, rabbits then drop off the pace or stop altogether. Since rabbits are not trying to win the race, officials believed they should not be allowed to compete, and therefore, the IAAF put in place a rule disallowing world records achieved with the use of a rabbit. Although this rule remained on the books for half a century, officials found it difficult to determine a runner's intent. By the early 1950s, the rule was ignored and has since been rescinded.

Similarly, a rule that international track officials tried to impose on marathon runners in 1915 never caught on. The IAAF put in a rule banning marathon runners from receiving refreshments during a race. Recognizing that such a rule would put the athletes' health at risk, however, U.S. track officials refused to adopt the rule and it was withdrawn without ever being enforced.

There have been some changes in the distance events included at the international level, however. In the 1912 Olympics, the 5,000 meters and 10,000 meters were added to the original 800 meters, 1,500 meters, and marathon. Also, in the early twentieth century, a variety of races were designed to combine distance running and jumping over obstacles. A number of steeplechase and cross-country events were tried in the Olympics, but all eventually were abandoned. The only survivor was the 3,000-meter steeplechase, introduced at the 1920 Olympics. This event requires 28 jumps over 3-foot high hurdles, plus 7 jumps over a 12-foot long water pit.

Walks, on the other hand, have been a source of controversy ever since they were added to the Olympics in 1956. The rule requiring a walker to have one foot in contact with the ground at all times is easy to break and a nightmare to enforce over an entire 20- or 50-kilometer course. Numerous Olympic walk medalists have been disqualified for breaking this rule, including Mexico's Bernard Segura, whose first-place finish at the 2000 Olympics in Sydney was erased. Judges are now considering putting a device on participants' shoes to signal when the walker is not in continuous contact with the ground.

Event Rules: The Throws

Although the discus throw dates back to ancient Greece, those early Olympic participants would not recognize today's competition. For the Greeks, the discus throw was more of an artistic event than a strength contest—they considered form and accuracy more important than distance. Although those who practiced the art in Europe in the eighteenth century competed for distance, they retained the ancient Greek form of throwing.

The Americans at the 1896 Games, however, knew nothing of Greek traditions. While the Europeans uncorked their throws from a standing position, the Americans whirled around two or three times to gain momentum for their throws. This gave them more distance, and the Europeans were forced to copy the style in order to compete. In the 1940s, discus competitors gained even more momentum by spinning around from the back to the front of the eight-foot circle before unleashing their throws.

The javelin was another ancient event that first appeared in the modern Olympics in 1906, and became subject to changing rules. By 1986, international competitors were throwing the spears so far that officials feared for the safety of spectators. In response to this concern, the balance point and grip were moved forward 10 centimeters and the tail was made narrower to cut down on distance. The javelin must be released above the shoulder and must break turf for the throw to count.

In 1896, the Greeks also included an event called "putting the weight." The name was soon changed to the shot put, as the weight was a 16-pound steel ball in the form of a cannon shot. In the early days, shot-putters sidestepped across the throwing circle to gain momentum for their throws. In 1951, however, Parry O'Brien, a student at the University of Southern California, experimented with a new technique. He began with his back to the throwing area, crouched deeply on his back foot, and then hopped forward, spun, and sprang up in the air all in one motion. "I met with a great deal of skepticism on the part of the so-called experts of the day," says O' Brien.[11] But after he won both the 1952 and 1956 Olympics, virtually all shot-putters adopted his style.

After shot-putter Parry O'Brien won the 1952 and 1956 Olympics, most shot-putters adopted his unusual style.

The hammer throw is the only addition to the throwing events from the first Olympics. This event, in which competitors sling an 8-pound steel ball on a wire leash, entered the Olympics in 1900.

Rules for Jumping Events

Track and field during the nineteenth century offered a hodgepodge of jumping events. The early Olympics included both standing and running jumps, and various international meets included several combinations of hops, steps, and jumps. The variety of events caused confusion until a 1913 ruling by the IAAF that limited jumping competition to four events: the high jump, long jump, triple jump (hop, step, and jump), and pole vault. Ironically, the man who was probably the greatest all-around leaper of all time never participated in any of these events at the Olympics. From 1900 to 1908, Ray Ewry won a total of ten Olympic gold medals in the standing high jump, standing long jump, and standing triple jump, all of which were discontinued.

The greatest technological innovation in jumping has been in the landing areas. At the turn of the century, high jumpers and even pole vaulters landed in sand or sawdust. Since these offered only scant protection, jumpers had to jump in such a way that they could land on their feet to avoid injury. The introduction of foam rubber in the 1960s and air cushion pads soon afterward eliminated most of the concern over injuries.

Ten-time Olympic gold medal winner Ray Ewry competes in the standing high jump at the 1908 Olympics. This event was later discontinued.

The high jump, however, has seen more alterations in rules and technique than any other track and field event. Early high jumpers hurdled the bar. The western roll, in which jumpers twisted their bodies sideways over the bar rather than hurdled it, was originated by George Horine in 1912. A rule prohibiting headfirst diving over the bar produced a huge controversy in 1932. Babe Didriksen lost the gold medal to Jean Shiley when her last jump was disqualified as a dive. Such judging disputes were eliminated when the diving prohibition was lifted in 1938.

POLE VAULT CONTROVERSIES

The rules pertaining to the poles used in the pole vault have always been loose. For the most part, competitors were free to use whatever material they wanted in their poles. During the nineteenth century, steel-pronged oak poles were popular. Bamboo poles took over in the early twentieth century.

As science and technology developed new materials, the poles began to differ widely. Using a bamboo pole, Dutch jumper Cornelius Warmerdam accomplished a world record of 15 feet, 7 3/4 inches in 1946, a mark that stood for fifteen years, though he never won an Olympic gold medal. In the 1950s, U.S. vaulters used light steel and aluminum poles to gain Olympic victories. Meanwhile, in 1956, Greek pole vaulter Georgias Roubanis and U.S. decathlete Bob Matthias experimented with a new material —fiberglass.

Pole vaulter Bob Seagren during the 1972 Olympic tryouts.

In 1962, American John Uelses used a high-density fiberglass pole to set a world record of 16 feet, 3/4 inches. Some critics protested that Uelses' record should not count because the fiberglass pole gave him an advantage over pole-vaulters who did not have access to this type of material. But, as the New York Times quoted one top vaulter, in Track & Field: The New York Times Encyclopedia of Sports, "You can't have the three or four records; one for hickory, one for bamboo, one for ash, and still another for fiberglass."

For the most part, track officials stayed away from the regulation of poles, preferring to let the athletes gravitate to whatever material worked best. Fiberglass did, in fact, prove to be far superior to other materials because it bent and then snapped the vaulters into the air. In just over a year, vaulters using that type of pole raised the world record by more than a foot.

On July 25, 1972, the IAAF suddenly banned a new high-density fiberglass "Cata-pole" that U.S. vaulter Bob Seagren had used to set a world record of 18 feet, 5 3/4 inches earlier that year. After Seagren and others protested vehemently that there was no legal basis for this action, the ban was lifted on August 27. Olympic officials then changed their minds yet again on August 30, just a day before the competition. Seagren's four favorite poles were confiscated, forcing him to scramble for borrowed poles on which he had never practiced. Seagren, the defending champion in the event, ended up losing to East Germany's Wolfgang Nordwig. His fury over this arbitrary treatment was not helped when the IAAF turned around and made the poles legal again four weeks later. The IAAF has since backed away from regulation of poles.

Dick Fosbury won a gold medal in the high jump at the 1968 Olympics using a technique dubbed the "Fosbury Flop," which most jumpers later imitated.

In 1967, U.S. jumper Dick Fosbury astounded spectators by running up to the bar, arching his back over it, and then finally lifting his legs over it. Track purists made fun of the "Fosbury Flop," as the technique became known, until Fosbury won a gold medal with it at the 1968 Olympics. Since that time, most high jumpers have adopted Fosbury's style.

The long jump and triple jump have remained much as they were in the first modern Olympics. The only significant alterations have been the introduction of synthetic runway surfaces, and electronic measuring devices for both distance and fouls.

The pole vault is thought to have originated centuries ago in the Netherlands, where farmers used poles to help them vault over drainage ditches. It is the only track and field event in which the athletes use something other than their bodies to help them accomplish their goal. Because so much depends on the qualities of the man-made poles, this event has produced more technological innovations than any other track and field event, along with a great deal of controversy.

Although such changes and innovations are common, track and field remains a sport with some of the oldest traditions of any athletic contest. For this reason, track and field consistently provides fans and competitors with some of the most exciting events the world of sports has ever seen.

CHAPTER 3

Breaking the Gender Barrier

The ancient Greeks considered sports to be in the realm of manly activities. During their first Olympic Games, the contestants generally performed in the nude, and the arena in which the games were held were off limits to women. There is evidence that at one time, women found in attendance could be put to death. But even though the Olympic Games were the exclusive privilege of men, the Greeks acknowledged that it was beneficial for women to partake in physical exercise, although on a far more limited scale. Thus, they set aside a similar, smaller scale version of the Olympics for women, focusing on track and field events, which they held every five years.

Despite his idealistic claim that the Olympics was "to be for everyone with no discrimination on account of birth, caste, financial standing, or occupation," [12] Baron de Coubertin continued the Greek ban on women participants in his Olympics, although he did lift the prohibition against female spectators. Thus, all official participants in the 1896 Olympics were male.

The rebirth of the Olympics, however, took place at a time when women's athletic contests were gaining acceptance in both Europe and the United States. Women made such strides in breaking into the traditional male domain of sports during that time that one woman wrote, "With the single exception of the improvement in the legal status of women, their entrance into the realm of sports is the most cheering thing that has happened to them in the century just past." [13]

Although Olympic officials permitted female spectators at the 1896 Olympics, women were not allowed to compete in the Games.

Vassar College, in particular, promoted participation in women's track and field in the United States. Because the college was the primary institution in the country concerned with women's track and field records, the vast majority of those marks during the late nineteenth century were held by Vassar students. As late as 1905, Vassar women held ten of the fifteen recognized U.S. records in women's track and field.

The growing popularity of women's sports put constant pressure on de Coubertin and other Olympic organizers to include them in the Olympics, beginning with the very first competition. According to unsubstantiated but persistent reports, in 1896, a Greek woman named Melpomene petitioned the Game's organizers for permission to enter the marathon. When her request was denied, she hid herself off to the side of the starting line and ran unseen parallel to the competitors. Once the field passed out of sight of the race officials at the start, she moved onto the race course.

A number of male runners dropped out of the race from overheating and exhaustion, and collapsed under shade trees. They were surprised to see a woman run past them, slowly but doggedly. Melpomene arrived at the Olympic stadium in Athens an hour and a half behind the winner, Spiridon Louis. When Olympic officials refused to allow her onto the track to finish the course, she ran her last lap outside the stadium.

Breaking Olympic Barriers

The Olympics began to include women's events such as tennis and golf beginning in 1900, but these were considered more courtship activities, similar to parlor games, rather than competitive sport. The majority of international track and field officials con-

tinued to fight women's participation every step of the way. According to Janet Woolum, despite the efforts of college educators, "women who participated in sports early in the twentieth century . . . generally did so outside the strict confines of proper behavior set by society."[14] The principle organizer of the 1904 Olympics in St. Louis, James Sullivan of the United States, reflected the majority view when he rejected women's athletics as "morally a questionable experience for women."[15]

By 1916, attitudes had loosened enough that even the traditionally conservative U.S. Amateur Athletic Union began sanctioning a

Archery was one of the few early Olympic events that welcomed female participants.

few women's track and field competitions. The International Olympic Committee (IOC), however, continued to ignore the sport even though it had sanctioned a similar type of competitive activity, swimming, in 1912.

Believing that the best way to influence Olympic officials was via strong organization, Alice Milliat of France founded the Federation Sportive Feminine Internationale in 1921. This group initiated a Women's Olympics in 1922 that shadowed the men's competitions. Meanwhile, in the United States, the Amateur Athletic Union moved forward another step by sponsoring its first national outdoor track and field championships for women, held in West Newark, New Jersey, in 1923.

Although these sports organizations put increasing pressure on the International Olympic Committee to include women's track and field events, de Coubertin stood firm. To his dying day, he tried to keep the Olympics as free of women as possible, particularly the sport of track and field. "Let women do all the sports they wish—but not in public," he pleaded.[16]

De Coubertin, however, could not last forever. After he retired as president of the IOC before the 1928 Olympics, his successor, Count Henri de Baillet-Latour of Belgium, tried to uphold de Coubertin's principles but did not have the same clout as the old Olympic founder. Over his objections, the IOC approved five women's track and field

American Elizabeth Robinson wins the women's 100-meter race at the 1928 Amsterdam Olympics.

THE FLYING HOUSEWIFE

Born in 1918, in Baarn, Netherlands, Fanny Blankers-Koen came from a family that encouraged her to take part in athletics. As the 1940 Olympics approached, the Dutch had high hopes that this young star could capture a gold medal in at least one of the many events in which she excelled. Then, five months before the Olympics were to take place, Adolf Hitler's German army roared through Poland. Whereas the ancient Greeks suspended their wars in order to hold the Olympics, the modern nations did just the opposite. World War II forced the cancellation of both the 1940 and 1944 Games.

It seemed that Blankers-Koen would never get the opportunity to demonstrate her talents to the world. Furthermore, at about the time the war finally ended in 1945, she became pregnant with her second child. No one imagined that a mother of two could compete in track and field at a world class level. Most doubted it was physically possible for her to regain her speed even if her duties as a mother were not too time-consuming for her to train.

Dutch athlete Fanny Blankers-Koen won the 80-meter hurdles at the 1948 Olympics.

Blankers-Koen, however, was not ready to give up the sport she loved. Everyday, she rode her bike to the track with her two children sitting in a basket strapped over the rear wheel. While the children played in the sand of the long jump pit, their mother worked out under the direction of their father.

When the Olympics resumed in London in August of 1948 after a twelve-year absence, Blankers-Koen stole the show. Running on a muddy track, she won the 100-meter dash, the 80-meter hurdles, the 200-meter dash, and anchored the Dutch team to a first place in the 4 x 100 relay. The most amazing part of her record-setting Olympic performance was that she did not even take part in what many considered her best events. (Prior to the Olympics, Blankers-Koen had posted world records in both the long jump and high jump.)

During her career, Blankers-Koen won fifty-eight Dutch national championships and set thirteen world records in a total of six different events. Had the Olympics not been derailed due to World War II, she likely would have collected more gold medals than any other woman in Olympic history.

events for the 1928 Olympic program in Amsterdam: the 100 meters, 800 meters, high jump, discus, and 4 x 100 relay.

The Infamous 800 Meters

The 800-meter race proved to be a public relations disaster. Other than the Germans, who were more accepting than most nations of female athletes, few women of that time had experience running so long a race. They were unwitting victims of the strategy that Lina Radke and her German teammates devised for winning the gold medal. Radke's teammates took off at a blistering pace. The competition strained mightily to keep up with them, while Radke trailed comfortably behind. The front-runners eventually ran themselves into exhaustion and Radke was able to sprint past them at the end with an impressive time of 2 minutes, 16.8 seconds.

Almost all the women had pushed themselves to the very limits of their endurance and all completed the race. Yet instead of being impressed by the women's heroic efforts, many people were shocked and appalled. "Below us on the cinder path were eleven wretched women," wrote one American sports columnist, "five of whom dropped out before the finish, while five collapsed after reaching the tape."[17]

People claiming to be medical experts weighed in with their judgment that the finish of the 800-meter race was merely proof that women were not physically designed for sports. Some critics claimed that women

athletes ran an increased danger of developing heart trouble. Donald A. Laird wrote in *Scientific American* that "feminine muscular development interferes with motherhood."[18] Even other women athletes expressed second thoughts about how far women should go in their pursuit of sports opportunities. Betty Robinson, a sprinter who won the U.S.' first gold medal in women's track and field at the 1928 Games, said in an interview that women were not built for races as long as 800 meters.

Although reliable medical research showed no ill effects for women from strenuous physical exercise, this fact was ignored amid the controversy. Also ignored was the fact that just four years earlier, the men's 800 meters ended in a similar fashion. After placing third, Hyla Stallard of Great Britain had collapsed and remained unconscious for half an hour without attracting any particular notice. The difference, according to Fred Steers, Chairman of the Women's Athletic Committee of the AAU, was that "the effect and fatigue of competition does not conform to the American ideals of womanly dignity and conduct. It does not lead to the promotion of sport, but on the contrary, because of its effect on the spectators, is detrimental."[19]

Backlash and Boycott

The furor over the 800-meter event touched off a backlash against women's participation in track and field. Not only did the International Olympic Committee vote to drop women's track and field from the program, but IOC president Baillet-Latour tried to eliminate all women's events. He was even supported by a number of other organizations, including the Women's Division of the National Amateur Athletic Union in the United States. Even the IAAF yielded to public outrage and banned all long races from women's competition.

Within all those groups, however, there were individuals stubbornly committed to promoting sports competition for women. The most influential of these was Gustave Kirby, who became president of the AAU prior to the 1932 Olympics in Los Angeles. With the support of an unlikely ally, U.S. Olympic administrator Avery Brundage, Kirby declared that the U.S. men's team would boycott the track and field events if women were not allowed to compete.

IOC officials recognized this as a serious threat to the future of the Olympics. If the host team, which also boasted many of the world's best track and field athletes, sat out the showcase competition of the games, the entire affair would be a financial and public relations bust. Despite objections from France, England, Italy, and Hungary, the IOC backed down. The 1932 Olympics featured six events for women, adding the 80-meter hurdles and the javelin. But officials held their ground on their objections to endurance competition and refused to sanction any race for women longer than 100 meters.

Babe Didriksen (right) races to a gold medal finish in the women's 80-meter Olympic hurdle competition. As recently as the early 1930s, Olympic officials refused to sanction races longer than 100 meters for women.

Tarnished Image

Some of the women gave spectacular performances at the 1932 Olympics, yet even they failed to dislodge widespread public prejudice against women athletes. Track and field stars, such as sprinter Stella Walsh, and all-around performer Babe Didriksen, drew criticism because they did not conform to the standards of feminine appearance or behavior.

Avery Brundage was one of those offended by the so-called "muscle molls" of sport. Once a supporter of women's Olympic competition, he changed his mind after taking control of the IOC. "You know, the ancient Greeks kept women out of their athletic games," he told reporters. "They wouldn't even let them on the sidelines. I'm not so sure but they were right."[20]

Sportswriters, for the most part, ignored women's athletic competitions. Bert Nelson, a writer for *Track & Field* magazine, explained why in response to a complaint about the lack of coverage. "Personally, I can't get very excited about girlish athletes . . . I seem to feel about the same as 99 per cent of the track fans I know."[21]

Growing Participation

Despite the opposition of Brundage and others, women's participation in the Olympics grew steadily. Following a twelve-year break caused by World War II, the 1948 Olympics offered an expanded slate of women's track

Fanny Blankers-Koen crosses the finish line first at the 1948 Olympics, which featured an expanded schedule of women's events.

BABE DIDRIKSEN

Mildred "Babe" Didriksen refused to concede anything to males in the area of physical activity. Louise Tricard, in *American Women's Track & Field*, quotes Didriksen as saying, "Before I was even in my teens I knew exactly what I wanted to be when I grew up. My goal was to be the greatest athlete that ever lived."

Born in Texas in 1914, Didriksen pursued that goal relentlessly. During her high school career, she competed in baseball, basketball, volleyball, golf, tennis, and swimming. She once hit five home runs in a single baseball game, which brought comparisons to major league home run king Babe Ruth, and earned her the lifelong nickname of Babe.

After high school she led an amateur basketball team formed by her employer to three Amateur Athletic Union (AAU) finals and one national title. Following that, she turned her sights on track and field. On July 16, 1932, at the combined AAU nationals and U.S. Olympic trials held at Northwestern University, she single-handedly beat all the other track teams in the nation. Feeding on the enthusiasm of 5,000 amazed fans, she rushed from event to event—eight in all. In stifling heat, she set world records in the 80-meter hurdles and javelin, and tied the world record in the high jump. She also finished first in the shot put, long jump, and baseball throw, and took fourth in the discus. Unfortunately, Olympic rules prohibited women from competing in more than three events. Didriksen reluctantly settled for the three in which she had set world records.

Didriksen, dubbed by the press as "The Texas Tornado," irritated and offended her teammates with her tobacco chewing and bragging. "I think a lot of girls found her behavior a little beyond how they thought a young lady should act," said her high jump

Babe Didriksen at the 1932 Olympics.

rival, Jean Shiley, quoted in Lewis H. Carlson and John J. Fogarty's *Tales of Gold*. "Nobody did anything better than she did. I don't care if it was swallowing goldfish; she would have to swallow more goldfish than anyone else."

Didriksen was able to back up her boasts, winning both the 80-meter hurdles and the javelin in the 1932 Olympics; however, she lost the high jump to Shiley because of a controversial disqualification. She likely would have won more Olympic medals than any other person in history had she not been banned from future competition because of a paid advertisement in 1935. That incident sent her into the world of professional golf, where she enjoyed a stellar career.

and field events. Included were the 200 meters and an event previously dismissed as something entirely unfit for women: the shot put. Twelve years later, the long-standing misconceptions about women and endurance events finally began to give way under a mountain of contradictory evidence. The 1960 Rome Olympics finally broke the thirty two-year ban on track races longer than half a lap, by bringing back the infamous 800-meter run. Four years later, a grueling five-event competition known as the pentathlon was added to the Games. In 1972, a 1,500-meter race, roughly the equivalent of a mile, took its place among women's competition. Four years later, Tatyana Kazankina of the Soviet Union drove another nail in the coffin of the feminine frailty myth by easily capturing the gold medal in both the 800 meter and 1,500 meter. In 1984, the women's pentathlon was expanded into an even more strenuous test— the heptathlon, which consisted of the 100 meters, high jump, shot put, 200 meters, long jump, javelin, and 800 meters.

Marathon: Final Frontier

The greatest hurdle in the struggle for recognition of women's track and field capabilities was the legendary endurance test, the marathon. During the 1960s, a few daring women attempted to get around the universal rule that women could not run marathons. In 1966, Roberta Gibb Bingay, disguised in a hooded sweatshirt, ran in the Boston Marathon, the oldest and most prestigious

annual marathon in the world. Although not officially entered, she finished ahead of more than half the field. A year later, Katherine Switzer entered the race under the name "K. Switzer." Observers spotted her early in the race, however, and one particularly gruff official tried to shove her off the course. Although he was thwarted by Switzer's male bodyguard, photographs of the incident incensed sports fans who were upset that the official had tried to bully Switzer off the course. Various marathon races began allowing women to participate, and a few even began holding a special competition for women runners.

The IOC, however, held out until the 1984 Olympics. There, the hot, humid air of Los Angeles provided a daunting challenge for those who wanted to prove women could safely participate in the most exhaustive of endurance runs. One who accepted the challenge was Joan Benoit of Cape Elizabeth, Maine. Benoit had started running as a senior in high school to get back into shape after suffering a broken leg while skiing. She continued training in college and won the women's competition in the 1983 Boston Marathon in only her second try at marathoning, with a world record time of 2 hours, 22 minutes, 43 seconds.

Upon hearing that the marathon was to be included in the 1984 Olympics, she quit her job as a coach and went into full-time training. Seventeen days before the U.S. Olympic trials, however, she had to have arthroscopic surgery on her knee. Although she came back to win the trials, she was not favored to win the Olympics.

Just fourteen minutes into the Olympic marathon, Benoit made a move that shocked everyone. While other competitors ran conservatively to keep from wilting in the oppressive heat, Benoit shot out to a commanding lead after just three miles. With steely determination, she held the lead for the next twenty-three miles. As she entered the stadium for one final lap of the track, she told herself, "Listen, just look straight ahead, because if you don't you're going to faint."[22]

Benoit's time of 2:24:52 would have shocked the officials of the 1928 Olympics who declared that an 800-meter race was beyond the ability of women. Not only was it faster than any of the men marathon runners in the 1928 Olympics, but she would

Joan Benoit celebrates her victory in the 1984 women's Olympic marathon; 1984 was the first year a women's marathon was included at the Games.

OVERCOMING ADVERSITY

Some of the most inspiring stories of athletic accomplishment concern athletes who overcame exceptional obstacles on their road to success. Few athletes have shown more courage than Wilma Rudolph and Gale Devers. At the age of four, Rudolph contracted several devastating illnesses, double pneumonia, scarlet fever, and polio, that left her partially paralyzed. Doctors predicted she would never be able to walk normally. But the rural Tennessee native worked hard to overcome her disability, hopping around on her weak leg to strengthen it. By the age of seven, she was walking, and at twelve she could run faster than most children her age.

During her career as an all-state basketball player at Burt High School, the school organized a track team. Rudolph discovered she was even better at sprints than at basketball. Under the guidance of Tennessee State University's legendary coach, Ed Temple, she made the 1960 U.S. Olympic team.

At the Rome Olympics, Rudolph easily captured gold medals in the 100 meters, 200 meters, and 4 x 100 relay, completing her transition from a partially disabled youngster to one of the most graceful sprinters in the world.

Likewise, nearly thirty years later, Gail Devers of Seattle, Washington, set a U.S. record in the 100-meter hurdles, and then was stricken with a severe case of Graves' disease. Radiation treatment for this thyroid condition caused her feet to swell so badly that doctors feared they would have to amputate both of them.

Devers fought through the disease and made her way back to the track and won gold medals in the 100-meter dash in both 1992 and 1996. As quoted in Janet Woolum's *Outstanding Women Athletes*, Devers told reporters, "I'm a stronger, more determined person because of it. After conquering Graves' disease, I know there is no hurdle I can't get over."

have finished a mile and a half in front of that year's gold medal winner. Her performance, and those of the other female runners who finished close behind her, put to rest for all time the old myths that strenuous athletic competition was for men only.

No More Question

At the dawn of the twenty-first century, the debate over the desirability of women in track and field competition was dead and buried. Women had become as active in international competition as men. With the addition of the pole vault, hammer throw, and 20-kilometer walk in 2000, the Olympics women's program became identical to the men's with the exception of only the steeplechase, the 50-kilometer walk, and the substitution of the heptathlon for the men's decathlon, and the 100-meter hurdles for the 110-meter hurdles. Perhaps the most telling example of society's change in attitudes toward women in Olympic competition has been the television ratings. Beginning in 1992, television networks found that well over half the viewers of their Olympic coverage were women.

In fact, the star of the track and field competition at the 2000 Olympic Games in

Sydney, Australia, was a woman, Marion Jones of the United States. As a young girl, Jones had written a promise to herself that she would one day be an Olympic champion. The Los Angeles native worked hard to achieve that goal, only to miss the 1996 Olympics because of a foot injury. She fought back from that disappointment to qualify for the U.S. team in five events: the 100, 200, long jump, 4 x 100 relay, and 4 x 400 relay. Experts conceded that Jones was right when she declared, "I have a chance to achieve something no one else has ever done—win five gold medals in track and field in a single Olympics."[23]

Jones fell short in her ambitious goal. A poor baton exchange between her teammates doomed the 4 x 100 relay team to

Marion Jones rejoices after winning the women's 100 meters by the widest margin in half a century of competition.

JACKIE JOYNER-KERSEE

Jackie Joyner came out of extreme poverty in a tough section of East St. Louis, Illinois, where she was born on March 3, 1962. Douglas Collins, in *Olympic Dreams*, quoted her older brother Al as saying of their childhood, "I remember Jackie and me crying together in a back room in that house, swearing that we were going to make it. Make it out."

It was athletics that helped Jackie get out, as she earned a basketball scholarship to UCLA. She accepted, on the condition that coaches also allow her to participate in track and field, where she was a four-time national junior champion in the pentathlon. Under the coaching of Bob Kersee, whom she eventually married, she won the NCAA heptathlon title (a seven-event competition that consists of the 100-meter hurdles, high jump, shot put, 200-meter dash, long jump, javelin, and 800-meter run) in 1982, with a record 6,088 points. In the winter of 1984, she qualified for the U.S. Olympic team in both the heptathlon and long jump. After losing the gold medal in the heptathlon by the narrowest of margins to Austria's Glens Nunn, Joyner-Kersee was more driven than ever to succeed. At the Goodwill Games in Moscow on July 7, 1986, she not only broke the world heptathlon record but also became the only woman to score more than 7,000 points in the heptathlon.

Unlike many heptathletes, Joyner-Kersee never seemed to hit a plateau. She kept improving in all events until she was the undisputed queen of the event. During the four years between the Olympics, she won every heptathlon competition she entered. As the 1988 Games in Seoul, Korea, approached, many people wondered how high Joyner-Kersee could push the record. Although two of her rivals in that competition topped the previous Olympic mark, neither was ever close to contending for the gold medal which Joyner-Kersee won by nearly 400 points. Then she went out and won the long jump, the first American woman to do so in forty years. She easily repeated her heptathlon gold medal in 1992, which moved world-class high jumper Dwight Stones to declare in Joyner-Kersee's autobiography, *A Kind of Grace*, "There's no argument that she [Jackie] is the greatest female athlete of all time."

Jackie Joyner-Kersee, who some say is the greatest female athlete of all time.

third place, and four fouls in six jumps left her with a bronze in the long jump as well. Still, she breezed to victory in the 200, won the 100 by the widest margin in half a century of competition, and ran a blistering leg of the 4 x 400 relay to assure victory. With three impressive gold medals, two bronze, and a dazzling smile, she easily stood out as the most popular athlete of the competition. The days when a sports editor could claim that nobody cared about women competitors in track and field was but a distant memory.

CHAPTER 4

The Political Burden of Track and Field

Track and field is a highly individualized sport that allows athletes to match their skills and willpower in head-to-head competition against other athletes. Curiously, this basic competition among individuals has produced perhaps more political controversy than any other sport. Track and field's universal appeal means that athletes from nearly every nation on earth take part in the competition. Unfortunately, the athletes often find themselves caught in a larger competition. Sometimes this has taken the form of an ideological war between unfriendly nations. At other times, because of their high profile during the Olympic years, athletes become symbols, even pawns, of various political movements.

Nationalism Comes to the Olympics

Baron de Coubertin's goal in creating the Olympics was to bring athletes from all nations together to promote not only physical exercise, but international cooperation. The Games were barely a decade old, however, when they threatened to produce more international strife than cooperation. In 1908, New York City shot-putter Ralph Rose, the flag bearer for the U.S. team at the opening ceremonies, created a stir when he refused to dip the U.S. flag when passing in front of England's review stand. Many Americans supported his action, declaring that the U.S. flag dips for no one, and, indeed, U.S. Olympic athletes have followed that rule ever since.

But England took offense at what they perceived as Yankee arrogance. From there, relations between the U.S. and English teams deteriorated, producing bitter disputes, disqualifications, protests, and heated debates in a number of events.

Once nationalism crept into the Olympics, it was nearly impossible to root out. During the 1912 Olympics, the *New York Times* began publishing its own scorekeeping tables, adding up the medals that each country won to see which nation was the overall victor. Despite firm denunciations by the International Olympic Committee, keeping score of the medal competition between nations has become standard practice of newspapers throughout the world. The 1924 Olympics in Paris were also marred by fierce nationalism on the part of the French spectators, whose enthusiasm in support of their own athletes degenerated into rudeness toward foreign athletes. Such episodes provided fodder for a long-standing debate among sports officials over whether the Olympics were worth continuing.

At the 1908 London Olympics, U.S. shot-putter Ralph Rose angered his English hosts when he refused to dip the U.S. flag as he passed in front of England's review stand.

The Nazi Olympics

All previous incidents were minor compared to the nationalistic bonfires that scorched Olympic ideals almost beyond recognition in 1936. Just three years after Adolf Hitler gained power in Germany, the Olympics were due to open in that nation's capital city of Berlin. Hitler and his followers viewed the Olympics as an opportunity to advance their philosophy that the "Aryan race"—white, northern Europeans—was superior to other peoples on earth. A directive from the German government proclaimed, "There has never before been developed a propaganda campaign equal to that of the Olympic Games."[24] By heavily promoting the recruitment and training of its athletes, Germany hoped to dominate the competition. A steady stream of German athletes taking the victory stand would provide strong visual proof of Aryan superiority.

Germany's intentions were so transparent that many Americans called on U.S. athletes to boycott the Games. U.S. Olympic official Jeremiah Mahoney agreed, saying, "I believe that for Americans to participate in the Olympics in Germany means giving American moral and financial support to the Nazi regime, which is opposed to all that Americans hold dear."[25] Despite this opposition, the U.S. officials, by a slim majority only, voted to send a team—although a number of individual athletes boycotted on their own.

As it turned out, the U.S. track and field team made a shambles of Hitler's intended demonstration of racial superiority. Although, according to Olympic fact compiler David Wallechinsky, "The Nazis had portrayed Negroes as inferior, taunting the United States for relying on 'black auxiliaries,'"[26] the African American athletes had the last laugh. Hitler abruptly halted his ritual of personally congratulating track and field victors when black U.S. high jumpers Cornelius Johnson and David Albritton placed first and second in one of the early competitions. Black sprinter Jesse Owens proved to be the star of the Games, winning four gold medals, and other blacks, such as sprinter Ralph Metcalfe and 800-meter runner John Woodruff, won more than their share of medals.

Adolf Hitler gives the Nazi salute at the 1936 Olympic Games in Berlin.

JESSE OWENS

The man who single-handedly made a mockery of Hitler's claim of German racial superiority was Jesse Owens. Owens was born in Danville, Alabama, on September 12, 1913, the grandson of slaves and the son of sharecroppers.

Owens, quoted in David Wallechinsky's *The Complete Book of the Olympics*, once told reporters that the secret of his success was that "I let my feet spend as little time on the ground as possible." At the Big Ten Conference championship on May 25, 1935, Owens, running for Ohio State University, did just that. In what was perhaps the greatest single-day track and field performance ever, Owens broke the world record in the long jump, 200 meters, 220 yards, 200-meter hurdles, and 220-yard hurdles, and tied the world record in the 100 meters all within a span of forty-five minutes.

This performance should have warned Hitler that, despite Nazi disparagement of U.S. black athletes, Owens was going to be the star of the 1936 Berlin Olympics. Sure enough, Owens held off teammate Ralph Metcalfe to claim gold in the 100 meters, then breezed to an easy win in the 200 meters. The long jump was a different matter. Owens ran through the pit on a practice run only to learn the officials were counting that as his first jump. Rattled, he fouled on his second jump and was in danger of missing the finals. For safety's sake, he drew a line a foot behind the takeoff board so that he would be sure to get a legal jump. The strategy worked. Owens made the finals and in a thrilling battle with Germany's Luz Long, earned his third gold medal.

Owens's fourth gold, which came in the 4 x 100 relay, left a sour taste in his mouth. Owens was not scheduled to run. But at the last minute, U.S. coaches replaced sprinters Marty Glickman and Sam Stollner with

Sprinter Jesse Owens at the 1936 Olympics.

Owens and another team member. Glickman and Stollner happened to be the only two Jews on the team, and the move appeared to be a blatant pandering to Adolf Hitler's anti-Jewish policies.

To Hitler's frustration, the German fans made no secret of their admiration for Owens. More than 100,000 fans in the stadium cheered his victories enthusiastically, and German crowds mobbed him wherever he went.

In recent years, research has uncovered another, even more cynical Nazi manipulation of the Olympics. German sports editor Klaus Huhn was quoted as admitting, "From the beginning, the Olympics was a cover for secret military preparations."[27] Far from being an event to promote world peace, the Olympics gave the Nazis the justification for constructing an elaborate Olympic village that was a front for a major armaments facility that was prohibited by treaty.

The Cold War

Olympic historians have called the 1948 Olympics "the last of the innocent Games"[28] because it was free of the politics, financial dealings, and cheating scandals that lurked on its doorstep. It was followed by the 1952 Games in Helsinki, Finland, in which the Soviet Union rejoined the world of track and field after an absence of forty years. The Soviets' reasons for competing had more in common with their ideological enemies, the

In 1936, Jesse Owens captured four gold medals and was the star of the Berlin Games.

60

Nazis, than with those promoting sport as a means of international cooperation. Like the Nazis, the Soviets targeted the Olympics as a way to improve the morale of their people and demonstrate the superiority of their form of government. They undertook the most extensive program yet to promote sports, including offering government subsidies to successful athletes so they could concentrate on their events without having to work at other jobs. The government also created boarding schools where children with talent could focus on training for their sport.

The Soviet government made it clear that its aims were not the same as the camaraderie and friendly competition espoused by Olympic idealists. "All athletes competing in foreign countries are especially trained and are taught to compete in a fighting spirit," according to official government policy. "Competitions are not just sporting events. They carry a tremendous ideological and political charge; they demonstrate the aspirations of the Soviet people."[29] Huge banners bearing the words, "All world records must be taken by Soviet Athletes," fluttered over arenas throughout the country.[30]

This determined campaign took its toll on Soviet athletes such as Valery Kuts. Although the training program imposed on Kuts by his coaches helped him to win gold medals in the 5,000 meters and 10,000 meters in the 1956 Olympics, it also ruined his heart. Kuts was forced to retire in 1960 after suffering the first of four heart attacks.

At the 1956 Olympics, Russian athlete Valery Kuts won gold medals in the 5,000 and 10,000 meters.

East German Juggernaut

Many of the Soviets' Eastern European allies adopted similar government-sponsored track and field programs, much to the annoyance of Western nations, who clung to the ideal of amateur competition. By far, the most ambitious government push for athletic dominance came from the East

THE TARDY SPRINTERS

One of the most bizarre episodes in the intense U.S.–Soviet track and field competition of the Cold War took place in the 1972 Olympics in Munich, Germany. Traditionally, America's 100-meter sprinters were the best in the world. Eddie Hart continued this tradition by tying the world record of 9.9 seconds in the U.S. trials, followed closely by Rey Robinson. But after years of frustrating failure, the Soviets had developed a world-class sprinter of their own—Valery Borzov. The match-up between Borzov and the Americans was one of the most highly anticipated events of the Games.

Borzov and the Americans easily sailed through the morning qualifying round. Then the Americans left the stadium to relax before their next scheduled heat at 7 P.M. Later that afternoon, Robinson was watching a television monitor while waiting for a bus to take him to the stadium. He asked another spectator if that was a rerun of the morning heat but was told the event was live.

Robinson, Hart, and the third American runner, Robert Taylor dove into cars in a frantic rush to get to the stadium. Unfortunately, Robinson's and Hart's heats were over by the time they got there. Taylor made his race, which he had to run without warming up.

It turned out that the U.S. team was working off an eighteen-month old schedule that had since been revised. Coach Stan Wright tearfully took the blame. "I gave them the wrong time," he said, quoted by the *New York Times*. "It's my fault."

But the Americans were not the only ones confused. Borzov, also working from an outdated schedule, thought he would be running next in the evening. Fortunately for him, he stayed at the stadium and was able to get to the starting line when he learned of his mistake.

In the finals, Borzov easily won the gold medal, with Robert Taylor, America's third best sprinter, capturing the silver medal. Hart and Robinson were left pondering what might have been.

Germans. Beginning in the late 1960s, the East German government committed 2 percent of the nation's income to cultivating Olympic champions. Their program included unprecedented funding for research in sports medicine and coaching techniques. Sports experts monitored every phase of an athlete's development, including "computerized medical records of every individual athlete right down to the state of every individual metabolism, every daily nutritional need." [31]

The results were astounding, particularly in the area of women's athletics. In 1968,

East German women won two medals in track and field. By 1976, the small nation of nineteen million people completely dominated the competition. That year, at the Montreal Olympics, the East German women won nineteen medals, including golds in the 200 meters, 4 x 100 relay, 4 x 400 relay, long jump, javelin, and discus, and a sweep of the top three places in the pentathlon.

The end of the Cold War between the Soviet bloc and the Western nations at the end of the 1980s eased some of the nationalistic fervor at international track and field. Media coverage of the Olympics, however, continued to report medal counts of various nations, and fund-raising efforts for Olympic teams continued to appeal to patriotism, urging donors to give generously so that their nation could triumph at the Games.

Political Protests

The idea of using Olympic competition as a political stage for protest, rather than merely prestige, dates back to the 1920 Olympics in Belgium. Smarting from Germany's recent invasion of their country during World War I, the host Belgians excluded German athletes from the Games, in glaring contrast to the stated ideals of the Olympic movement.

Other than a barely noticeable partial boycott of the 1936 Olympics, no further protests of major importance impacted the world of track and field until the civil rights movement in the United States during the 1960s. During that decade, African American athletes struggled with the issue of whether to boycott the Olympics as a way of calling attention to problems of racial inequality in the United States.

In general, track and field stood far ahead of most major sports in accepting competitors of all races, thanks in part to de Coubertin's stated ideals of nondiscrimination. As early as 1904, black American George Page won bronze medals in the 200 meters and 400-meter hurdles. But ugly incidents occasionally erupted over the years. In 1938, John Woodruff was timed at 1:47.8 in an 880-yard race at a track in the South, bettering the world record by nearly two seconds. Two weeks later, officials announced that the track measured six feet short, and the record was disallowed. Woodruff was convinced the claim of a short track was bogus. "You know what went on down there," he fumed, many years later. "Those people got their heads together and decided they weren't going to give a black man [the] record."[32]

As the U.S. civil rights movement swung into high gear during the 1960s, black track stars felt an obligation to use their fame to stand up for poor, powerless victims of discrimination. In 1967, the U.S. Olympic Committee (USOC) enraged black athletes by leading a campaign to allow South Africa to return to the Olympics. South Africa had been banned in 1960 because its government mandated discrimination against blacks. After several nations threatened to join the black Americans in a boycott of the Olympics, officials reinstated the ban. The incident, however, reinforced the feeling among African Americans that they were being used to win medals for a nation that did not respect them. The fact that all the U.S. coaches and Olympic officials were white further fueled resentment.

Although the blacks finally rejected a boycott of the 1968 Olympic Games in Mexico City, a number of them felt compelled to make some sort of statement against racial discrimination. Among them were Tommie

Smith and John Carlos, two San Jose State University sprinters who were members of the Olympic Project for Human Rights. After placing first and third respectively in the 200-meter dash, Smith and Carlos took the victory stand in black socks. During the playing of the U.S. national anthem in honor of their win, they bowed their heads and each raised a black-fisted glove in the air. "It was a protest to show that what we had won was for all black people,"[33] explained Smith.

The IOC responded to what they perceived as a violation of the Olympic ideal of sportsmanship and international cooperation and ordered both men out of the Olympic village for the rest of the Games. Commentators such as Brent Musberger railed against the two, calling them "black-skinned storm troopers."[34]

Carlos pointed out the hypocrisy of his critics' claims that any political statements degraded the Olympics. "Why do you have

Gold and bronze medalists Tommie Smith (center) and John Carlos (right) bow their heads and give the black power salute to protest unfair treatment of blacks in the United States.

THE TRUE OLYMPIC IDEALS

Despite the political controversies and rampant nationalism that have plagued Olympic track and field competition, most of the competitors have adhered to the ideals of sportsmanship first envisioned by Olympic founders. German long jumper Luz Long, for example, risked the wrath of Adolf Hitler by openly encouraging and congratulating his rival, Jesse Owens, during the 1936 competition.

Perhaps the most striking example of intense, yet friendly competition in track and field took place in the 1960 Olympic decathlon. Rafer Johnson of the United States and C. K. Yang of Taiwan staged a furious battle in the grueling ten-event competition. Although the two lived an ocean apart and competed for different countries, Yang and Johnson were friends, having trained and competed as teammates while in college at UCLA.

Neither contestant gave an inch as the competition wore on. Yang was faster and more limber and he defeated Johnson in all the running and jumping portions of the event. Johnson, who was larger and stronger, more than made up for this with his prowess in the throwing events. With one event left, the 1,500 meters, Johnson held a narrow lead over Yang. He needed to stay within a few seconds of Yang to claim the gold.

Both runners poured out every last ounce of strength during that race. The relentless Johnson clung to Yang's heels and finished

Friends and competitors, Rafer Johnson (left) and C. K. Yang congratulate each other after placing first and second in the decathlon.

just four yards behind to win the gold by just 58 points, out of a total score of 8,392. Having dueled to the limit of human endurance, the two rivals collapsed into each other's arms, congratulating and consoling each other, their close competition only increasing their admiration for each other.

to wear the uniform of your country?" asked Carlos. "Why do they play national anthems? Why do we have to beat the Russians? What happened to the Olympic ideal of man against man?"[35]

The athletes, themselves, were generally sympathetic to Smith and Carlos. Over time, most of the world came to share their point of view. "In retrospect," says Olympic historian David Wallechinsky, "Smith and Carlos's gestures on the victory platform in Mexico City appear as eloquent expressions of nonviolent protest, while the reactions of the IOC and USOC come off as knee-jerk traditionalists."[36]

The Boycotts

The IOC's desperate attempt to stamp out political protest at the Mexico City games proved futile. In 1976, nearly an entire continent decided to take up the banner of conscience that Smith and Carlos had raised, and this time their actions dealt a telling blow to the Games.

The problem began earlier that year when New Zealand's national rugby team traveled to South Africa for a series of games, despite the fact that this violated the Olympic organization's rule banning athletic competition with that nation. Black African nations demanded that New Zealand be banned from the Olympics for this violation. When the IOC refused to take action against New Zealand, the African nations withdrew their teams.

The African boycott spoiled some of the most highly anticipated contests of the Montreal Games. Sports fans had been looking forward to the 1,500-meter battle between world record holder Filbert Bayi of Tanzania and his friend John Walker of New Zealand. Without Bayi present to set his usual blistering pace, Walker won a lackluster final in an embarrassingly slow time. Fans were also left wondering whether Finland's Lasse Viren, winner of the 5,000 meters and 10,000 meters could have withstood the fierce finishing kick of Ethiopia's Miruts Yifter. Furthermore, the boycott wiped out epic battles between 1972 gold medal winner John Akii-Bua of Uganda and the new American star Edwin Moses in the 400-meter hurdles, and Kenya's Mike Boit and Cuba's Alberto Juantorena in the 800 meters.

Four years later, an even more devastating boycott rocked the Olympics. In protest of the Soviet Union's invasion of Afghanistan, U.S. president Jimmy Carter ordered the U.S. Olympic team to boycott the 1980 Olympics in Moscow. Several U.S. allies joined the boycott. Again, many of the track and field events suffered from the absence of world-class runners, jumpers, and throwers. The top three hurdlers in the world, for example, were all from the United States. Any one of them could have beaten the winning Olympic 110-meter hurdle time of 13.39 seconds without any trouble.

The boycott plague continued for one more round, as the Soviets took their revenge by boycotting the 1984 Olympics in Los Angeles. Most of the Eastern European nations, including sports power East Germany, joined the boycott. Consequently, the field was so depleted in many events, particularly on the women's side, that the Olympics could hardly claim to be a world-championship competition.

Back to the Ideals

The twelve-year rash of boycotts finally wound down with the 1988 Games in Seoul, Korea. Except for a boycott of those games by Cuba that forced Javier Sotomayer, the world record holder in the high jump, to miss the competition, all the world's top track and field athletes participated. Even the decades-long political squabbling that kept the world's most populous country, China, from participating, finally ended. Having ousted its white supremacist government, South Africa was readmitted to the Olympics in 1992. As if in celebration of that fact, sports fans were treated to an inspiring battle in the women's 10,000 meter run that year between gold medal winner Derartu Tulce, a black

The African boycott at the 1976 Montreal Games left fans wondering whether Finland's Lasse Viren (right) would have still won his gold medals had he competed against Ethiopia's Miruts Yifter.

Ethiopian, and runner-up Elana Meyers, a white South African.

That did not, however, mean the end of political influence on track and field. Since the Olympics had continued to grow in prestige and influence throughout the world, they remained a vehicle for the promotion of passionately held political beliefs. During the 2000 Olympics in Sydney, Australia, for instance, billions of spectators were captivated by the emotional turmoil surrounding 400-meter star Cathy Freeman. Freeman was an Australian Aborigine, a culture that had been persecuted by white Australians for more than two centuries. In 1994, Freeman became a controversial figure in her native land when she jogged a victory lap after one of her wins, wrapped in the Aboriginal flag.

In 2000, however, Freeman carried the hopes and expectations of a nation that was desperate for a track and field victory on its

Wearing the Australian and Aboriginal flags, Cathy Freeman revels in her 400-meter victory at the 2000 Sydney Olympics.

home track. Nearly overwhelmed by this burden, she started off slowly in the 400-meter finals. But fueled by a deafening roar from the crowd, she summoned a late surge to pass Lorraine Graham of Jamaica. After breaking the tape, Freeman sat on the track, stunned by the magnitude of her accomplishment while all around her fans applauded, shouted, and wept tears of joy. Then she shared a victory lap with the crowd, wearing the Australian and Aboriginal flags tied together.

For many, it was a watershed moment, offering hope of breaking through Australia's bleak record in race relations. Australian writer Tom Kenneally commented, "I'm skeptical about the idea that sports changes things any more than poetry or fiction can do, but this is quite like when Jackie Robinson played major league baseball in America, and if any sports event can change things, this one has a chance."[37] Freeman's story not only affirmed track and field's combination of individual human perseverance and international competition but also proved how difficult it is to completely divorce the world of track and field from the burning issues of the day.

CHAPTER 5

Cheating: The Bane of Track and Field

Tough competitors are constantly on the lookout for some way to gain an advantage on their opponents. They train hard, toughen themselves mentally, and try to keep their bodies in prime shape with special diets and sleep regimens. But the drive to win sometimes sends top athletes over the line into the realm of cheating. Over the years, international track and field has been plagued with the problem of athletes bending or even breaking the rules in order to win. Sometimes the cheating has been ridiculously obvious, such as Fred Lorz's hitchhiking stunt in the 1904 marathon. Occasionally, the cheating has been easily remedied with a simple rule change: For example, after Russian high jumper Yuri Stepanov was found to have broken the world record using shoes

with two-inch high soles, rules were written limiting the size of a jumper's soles to a half inch. There have, however, been three areas in which cheating, or the suspicion of it, has posed enormous and long-lasting problems in the sport of track and field: professionalism, gender, and drugs.

Professionalism— A Dirty Word

For much of its history, track and field has wrestled with the problem of whether athletes should compete strictly for the love of competition, or whether they should be allowed to make money from their skills. Where the ancient Greeks stood on this issue is still an open question. Some historians insist that the Greeks made no distinction between amateurs and professionals and that Olympic champions were often richly rewarded. Other historians claim that the Greeks became furious when the pure sport of their Olympics was defiled by Roman professionals.

The revival of track and field in the nineteenth century occurred at a time when the upper classes in western society looked down on professional sports. As John Cumming notes, "Professionalism was abhorrent to the upper class in America, not only for the corruption and gambling which were attached to the sport, but also for the rough element of the participants."[38] The English were also op-

posed to the practice of performing sports for money and worried that their American counterparts were not. In fact, during the latter nineteenth century, attempts at track and field competitions between the United States and Great Britain frequently broke down because of British accusations that the other nation was cheating—that its champions were professionals.

Such accusations flew freely on both sides of the Atlantic. One of the top U.S. runners of the 1880s, Lawrence Meyers, was frustrated at false claims accusing him of being a professional. "There is a fellow named

The early promoters of the Olympics, including Baron de Coubertin (seated left), came from the upper classes and believed the athletes should be amateurs; competing for money, they thought, was in poor taste.

Angie who is a photographer, and wanted to take my picture to sell," reported Meyers. "I refused him. He was at an athletic meeting the other day, and gave it out that I had asked him what I was going to get out of it, etc., and wound up his remarks by saying, of course, I was a professional."[39]

The Olympics— Amateurs Only

Like many people of his class, Baron de Coubertin found the idea of participating in sport for money beneath contempt. Unlike most of his peers, however, de Coubertin recognized that the type of international competition that the Olympics promoted was beyond the reach of the average person. To remedy the problem, he promoted the idea of patrons offering to finance the competition expenses of athletes who were working class people.

The notion did not meet with much enthusiasm. For the most part, the upper classes promoting the Olympics liked the idea of keeping the lower classes out. According to author John Lucas, the Olympics' strict insistence on amateurs only was primarily "an ideological means to justify an elitist athletic system that sought to bar the working class from competition."[40]

Statements from its original organizers back up this conclusion that Olympic competition was reserved for the upper classes, and that the amateur requirement was a means of enforcing this. Even when trying to express

some of the nobler ideals of the Olympics, U.S. Olympic Committee representative W. M. Sloane let his prejudices show. In advocating for the Olympics, Sloane said, "The more the higher classes of different nations get to know one another, the less likelihood of their fighting."[41]

The most spectacular scapegoat of the amateurs-only policy was Jim Thorpe, the Native American whose gold medals at the 1912 Olympics were stripped after it was revealed that he had played a season of semi-pro baseball. But in the decade following Thorpe's disqualification, even fairly well-to-do athletes began to complain of the cost of participating in sports on a world class level. In 1920, the IOC finally gave permission for athletes to accept some forms of reimbursement for travel expenses and loss of income. Enforcing this provision, however, proved to be an enormous headache, requiring track and field officials to play the part of auditors.

Convicted of Professionalism

Ever zealous in rooting out any traces of professionalism, Olympic officials dealt harshly with athletes, even world class runners, caught bending the rules. One of the first high-profile cases was Jule Ladoumeigue of France, the world record holder in the 1,500-meter run, who was banned for accepting illegal payments from race sponsers five months before the 1932 Olympics.

After learning that Native American athlete Jim Thorpe had played a season of semi-pro baseball, Olympic officials stripped him of his gold medals.

The biggest scandal at those Games, however, was that of the "Phantom Finn," Paavo Nurmi. The carpenter's son who a *Chicago Tribune* reporter described as a "frail-looking man with the shining hair and legs of steel, trained in the bleak Finnish northland,"[42] was far and away the greatest distance runner of his era. From 1921 to 1931, Nurmi broke more than two dozen world records in sixteen events ranging from 1,500 meters to 20,000 meters. Carrying his trademark stopwatch, with which he measured his pace, the unflappable Nurmi won nine gold medals from 1920 to 1928. His most incredible feat was capturing both the 1,500 and 5,000 meters with less than an hour's rest between them in 1924.

Nurmi warmed up for the 1932 Olympics by setting a world record in the marathon that year. His quest to improve on his medal collection came to an abrupt end just three days before the Olympics, however, when Nurmi was found guilty of accepting excess expense money for appearances. The absence of one of track and field's top stars from the Los Angeles Games struck reporter

Westbrook Pegler as absurd. "Paavo Nurmi had been convicted of making some money out of his principle business in his life, [running] a charge which citizens of most countries would like to plead guilty of,"[43] wrote Pegler.

More victims, or cheaters, depending on one's point of view, soon joined Nurmi on the sidelines. A few months after achieving celebrity status as the star of the 1932

Olympics, Babe Didriksen allowed an automobile dealer to use her name, photograph, and a personal interview in an advertisement. Although she claimed she had not intended the photo and interview to be used in this way, it was a violation of the eligibility rules for both track and field and the Olympics. On December 5, 1932, the AAU declared, "By sanctioning the use of her name to advertise, recommend, and pro-

World-record setting runner Paavo Nurmi was barred from competing in the 1932 Olympics after he was found guilty of accepting excess expense money for appearances.

JIM THORPE

In 1950, the Associated Press voted Jim Thorpe as the greatest athlete of the half century. Although the Sac and Fox Indian from Oklahoma was a star athlete in college and played pro football and pro baseball, he was most proud of his accomplishments at the 1912 Olympics. Despite having never competed in the decathlon, Thorpe was such a tremendous athlete that he easily beat European champions Hugo Weislander of Sweden and Ferdinand Bie of Norway for the gold medal. Thorpe also took first place in the pentathlon—a five event competition that was soon eliminated from the Olympics.

A few months after Thorpe's triumph, however, a reporter stumbled upon the fact that Thorpe had played baseball in the Eastern Carolina League during the summer of 1909. Although he received only a few dollars for doing so, the sports governing bodies ruled that this made him a professional athlete and thus ineligible to participate in the Olympics. He was ordered to return his Olympic medals.

Thorpe was distraught over the incident, and he appealed to the IOC. The IOC and the AAU, however, still rejected his appeal and erased his name from the record books. According to friends, Thorpe never completely recovered from the pain of losing his medals.

In 1973, twenty years after Thorpe's death, the U.S. Olympic Committee recognized the injustice of the situation and restored Thorpe's amateur standing in track and field. Ten years later, the IOC followed suit and overturned his disqualification, reinstated his name in the record books, and returned to his family the medals that had meant so much to him.

Jim Thorpe (left) at the 1912 Olympics.

mote the sale of an automobile, Mildred (Babe) Didriksen had automatically disqualified herself for further participation as an amateur."[44]

In May of 1936, U.S. officials stunned the track world again when they accused Kansas runner Wes Santee of taking $1,500 above allowable expenses in seven meets

Officials found U.S. runner Wes Santee guilty of accepting illegal expense payments and banned him from further competition.

during 1935. At the time, Santee owned the fastest mile time in the United States at 4:00.5 and was one of the prime contenders in the quest to break the 4-minute mile. Santee protested his banishment from the sport and took his case all the way to the U.S. Supreme Court. The court ruled against him, however, and affirmed that the track federations were within their rights to ban him from further competition.

Beginning in the 1950s, the Soviet Union and other Eastern bloc countries began taking advantage of loopholes in the amateur status rules. Although their athletes were not technically paid, they received generous compensation. They were given jobs and titles that required no responsibilities, perks such as comfortable housing that was not available to average citizens, and were trained at government expense. Throughout the Cold War era, athletes from the United States and Western Europe complained bitterly about the state-sponsored professionals from Communist nations. However, in contrast to the strict enforcement of rules about expense account money, Olympic and international track and field officials ignored the issue.

Some Western athletes also learned how to bend the rules. In 1972, Lasse Viren did a victory lap of the Munich stadium, during which he made a point of prominently displaying his running shoes. Although he defended his actions by saying his feet hurt, Viren was the exclusive distributor of Tiger shoes in Finland, and his antics were seen by some observers as exploiting his Olympic win for financial gain.

Bring on the Pros

In the early 1970s, promoters attempted to bring track and field into the arena of professional sports. Such track stars as Olympic champions Lee Evans, Wyomia Tyus, Jim Ryun, and Kip Keino were lured to track circuits with prize money and the promise of large bonuses for breaking world records. The pro circuit struggled for a couple of years before dying out altogether in 1976. It failed, according to the *New York Times*, "because, ironically, the best amateur athletes could make more money by remaining amateurs and accepting illegal appearance money from promoters,"[45] a fact that demonstrated the hypocrisy of the Olympics' insistence on amateurism.

The rules on amateurism in track and field were so poorly enforced that the administrative bodies finally agreed to put an end to the practice altogether in the 1990s. Beginning with the 1992 Barcelona games, the Olympics scrapped all rules against professional athletes, finally eliminating the longest-running controversy in track and field history.

Sex Masquerades

There were other controversies, however. As women's events grew in prominence, suspicions grew that some of the competitors

STELLA WALSH'S SECRET

Stanislawa Walasiewicz, a Polish immigrant who shortened her name to Stella Walsh while growing up in Cleveland, Ohio, dreamed of winning an Olympic gold medal. But the world class sprinter could not find employment during the bleak days of the Great Depression in the 1930s. In desperation, she accepted a job working for the Polish embassy in the United States, on the condition that she compete for Poland in the Olympics. Walsh won the women's 100-meter dash at the 1932 Olympics, with what one reporter, quoted in David Wallechinsky's *The Complete Book of the Olympics*, referred to as "man-like strides," tying the world record of 11.9 seconds in the process. Four years later, Walsh tried to defend her title but was defeated by Helen Stephens of the United States. After witnessing Stephens run an astounding time of 11.5 seconds at those games, a Polish journalist accused Stephens of being a man.

Nearly half a century later, the truth of the matter came out, and it was not Stephens who was hiding the truth. In December of 1980 Walsh got caught in the crossfire of a robbery and was shot to death in a parking lot. An autopsy revealed that Walsh was, in fact, a man. Track officials have been uncertain ever since what to do about the eleven world records and two Olympic medals listed under her name.

Stella Walsh (right) congratulates Helen Stephens after losing to her in the 100-meter dash.

were not women at all. Whenever a woman dominated a particular event, especially if some of her physical features were not particularly feminine, accusations arose that she was a man masquerading as a woman to achieve victory.

The clouds of suspicion hovered most stubbornly over the Press sisters from the Soviet Union. During the 1960s, Tamara and Irene Press dominated their track and field events. Between them, they set twenty six world records and captured five gold medals.

In the 1964 Olympics, Irene proved herself the world's top all-around woman athlete by winning the pentathlon, while Tamara scored the unprecedented feat of winning both the women's shot put and discus. But as U.S. Olympic star Wilma Rudolph later commented, "I remember the Press sisters very well. In Rome, we used to be puzzled by their mannish appearance."[46]

Rumors about men masquerading as women athletes spread so widely that, following the 1964 Olympics, the IOC de-

Gold medal winners Tamara (left) and Irene Press from the Soviet Union dropped out of track and field competition after the IOC began requiring female athletes to take a chromosome test.

cided to take a drastic step to end the controversy: They began subjecting all women athletes to a chromosome test to determine their sex. In 1967, Polish sprint champion Ewa Klobukowska became the first international star to fail the chromosome test. The IOC immediately took away the bronze medal she had won in the 1964 Olympics.

Suddenly, but quietly, Irene and Tamara Press disappeared from track and field competition. Most track experts suspected their retirement had to do with the fact that they could not have passed the chromosome test. But they were never tested, so there was no concrete evidence to justify stripping them of their medals and records. Gender testing continues to this day and has eliminated further controversy over the sex of the female champions.

Steroids

The most recent and most widespread form of cheating in track and field has involved the use of performance-enhancing drugs. During the early years of the modern Olympics, drug use was not considered cheating. Marathon racers at the turn of the century were commonly given stimulants to help them overcome exhaustion. While the Olympic movement was still in its infancy, however, officials came to the consensus that the use of drugs was an attempt to gain an advantage over opponents by artificial means, a fact which was contrary to the spirit of sports.

Track and field remained virtually free from the taint of drug use until the 1950s, when certain drugs from a chemical family known as steroids were discovered to greatly increase muscle mass. Although the side effects of these drugs were unknown and eventually proved to range from changes in appearance (loss of hair in men, growth of facial hair in women), to possible health hazards (depression, increased risk of cancer, and heart disease), world-class track and field athletes began injecting themselves with steroids. According to Harold Connolly of the United States, an Olympic champion in the hammer throw, "I knew any number of athletes on the 1960 Olympic team who had so much scar tissue and so many puncture holes in their backsides that it was difficult to find a fresh spot to give a new shot."[47]

U.S. athletes initially took the lead in steroid use, but by the late 1960s, Eastern European athletes had more than caught up. The East German women's teams, which came out of nowhere to dominate the Olympics in the 1970s, fell under particularly heavy suspicion that they got their strength, not from training but from the pharmacy.

Policing Steroid Use

The IOC and the international track and field governing bodies all condemned the use of steroids and instituted drug testing to catch those who defied the steroid ban. In 1976, Danuta Rosani of Poland became the first Olympic track and field athlete disqualified for steroids when she failed her drug test after qualifying for the discus finals.

The problem that frustrated officials, however, was that steroid use was difficult to detect. Steroids accomplished their effect long before the actual major competitions, by which time little trace of them remained in the body. This meant that even rigorous testing for steroids could catch only the most blatant and ignorant users. Some sports medicine experts, such as East Germany's Manfred Ewald, hid behind this fact to justify the use of steroids for their athletes. "What cannot be detected cannot be considered against the rules,"[48] claimed Ewald.

Even though few athletes were caught, the rampant use of steroids among track and field athletes remained a poorly kept secret among participants.

The issue of steroids hid in the murky background of track and field until it was blasted out in the open at the 1988 Olympics in Seoul, Korea. There, 100-meter sprint champion Ben Johnson of Canada, who had destroyed the world record in capturing the gold medal, tested positive for steroids. Canadian officials, humiliated by their star athlete being disgraced before the world, ordered an inquiry into the matter. At first, Johnson and his coach denied using the banned substance. But eventually, Coach Charley Francis con-

Canadian sprinter Ben Johnson (right) lost his 1988 Olympic gold medal after he tested positive for steroid use.

BEN JOHNSON'S DISGRACE

Ben Johnson was a Jamaican immigrant who blossomed into Canada's greatest sprinter. But ever since he burst into prominence, his yellow-tinged eyes and muscle structure that would have put a comic book superhero to shame convinced opponents that he was taking steroids in massive amounts. Johnson denied it in a 1985 interview, quoted in David Wallechinsky's, *The Complete Book of the Olympics.* "Drugs are both demeaning and despicable and when people are caught they should be thrown out of the sport for good," Johnson said. "I want to be the best on my own natural ability and no drugs will pass into my body."

As the 1988 Olympics approached, Johnson charged past U.S. star sprinter Carl Lewis to lay claim to the title of The World's Fastest Human. At a competition in Rome in 1987, he rocketed down the track in a world record time of 9.83 seconds. Canada, which had not won an Olympic gold medal in track and field since 1932, hailed Johnson as a national hero.

During the 100-meter finals at the 1988 Seoul Olympics, Johnson burst out of the starting blocks as if shot out of a cannon. Even though Carl Lewis ran the race in a blistering 9.92 seconds, he was left far in his rival's wake. Johnson's time of 9.79 broke his own world record.

Two days later, however, while Canada was still basking in the victory, a urine test revealed the presence of the steroid stanozalol. Johnson was disqualified and his medal taken away. Although forty two athletes had been disqualified in Olympic competition prior to Johnson, none of them had been a star the caliber of Johnson.

Embarrassed Canadian track officials launched an inquiry into the situation. Intense questioning of Johnson's coach and doctor pried loose the truth that the sprinter had been taking steroids regularly since November 1981. His last injection had come twenty-six days before the Olympic finals. Johnson was banned from competition for two years, and never came close to matching his previous times.

fessed the obvious. However, he refused to admit that Johnson had done anything wrong. "I don't call it cheating," Francis said. "My definition of cheating is doing something nobody else is doing."[49] But in slapping Johnson with a two-year suspension from the sport, Canadian Judge Charles L. Durbin scoffed at such excuses. "The use of banned performance-enhancing drugs is cheating, which is the antithesis of sports."[50]

The Johnson episode cast a shadow of doubt on all track and field participants.

Any outstanding performance, such as Florence Griffith Joyner's blazing world record in the women's 200-meters at those same games, was met with skepticism. Those who played by the rules suffered the indignity of being condemned along with cheaters.

Further shame was heaped upon the track and field community when the Berlin Wall fell, and the closed Communist society of East Germany dissolved. An examination of the records exposed the East German sports program as a flagrant violator of the steroid ban. East German athletes, who claimed no knowledge of what their medical trainers had given them, were both furious and embarrassed at the revelation. "Medical men are the guilty people," fumed one world class athlete upon learning of the fraud. "They gave us things . . . we were never asked if we wanted them."[51]

Continuing Enforcement Problems

One case in particular demonstrated the complex problems that came with trying to isolate the cheaters from the clean athletes. In 1990, Butch Reynolds of the United States, the world record holder in the 400 meters, tested positive for steroids. He and his coaches fought the accusation vigorously, accusing the medical people of sloppy handling of test samples that confused Reynolds' sample with that of a German woman. Nonetheless, in December 1991, U.S. track governing bodies recommended that Reynolds be banned from the sport for life. Reynolds took his complaint all the way to the U.S. Supreme Court, which issued a ruling allowing Reynolds to compete at the 1992 U.S. Olympic Trials. International track officials breathed a sigh of relief when Reynolds failed to qualify in his event at those trials.

Enforcement of the steroid ban has continued to cause headaches in the Olympics. At the 1996 Games in Atlanta, nine athletes were found guilty of steroid use. When they appealed their cases to various sports governing bodies, however, all but two of their suspensions were overturned. Accusations surfaced that officials in some countries were covering up for top athletes who violated the steroid ban.

Most experts agreed that the only hope of cleaning up the sport entirely was for scientists to develop increasingly accurate tests for steroids, and for the international sports organizations to set up a system that would ensure strict, yet fair, enforcement of

Banned for life from track and field for alleged steroid use, sprinter Butch Reynolds (right) fought the accusation all the way to the U.S. Supreme Court.

82

antidrug rules. Better steroid tests appear to be the easy part. At the 2000 Olympics in Sydney, Australia, three dozen athletes were disqualified for steroid use, including world champion hammer thrower Mihaela Melinte of Romania, and dozens of others pulled out rather than submit to drug testing. A respected system of enforcement, however, has yet to be perfected.

The Challenge

World class athletes tend to be extremely competitive, and the riches and fame available to Olympic stars has made temptations to bend the rules stronger than ever. As U.S. track star Hal Connolly noted, "The overwhelming majority of international track and field athletes I know would take anything and do anything short of killing themselves to improve their athletic performance."[52] As track and field moves into the twenty-first century, officials will have to be constantly on the alert to determine when athletes give in to temptations and gain an unfair advantage over an opponent by cheating.

CHAPTER 6

Stars of Track and Field

Track and field competition has produced a long list of champions from all around the world who have thrilled fans with their accomplishments. Some, such as Jesse Owens, have not only been exceptional athletes but also major figures in world politics and culture. Others, including Babe Didrikson, Fanny Blankers-Koen, Jackie Joyner-Kersee, and Marion Jones have been pioneers in the establishment and advancement of women in sports.

In addition, track and field lore is filled with stories of fascinating personalities who have demonstrated both the physical skill and the determined spirit that lie at the heart of athletic competition. Each has raised the standards of achievement in their particular events far beyond the previous limits.

Roger Bannister

Many track and field buffs point to May 6, 1954, as the most significant day in the sport's history. On that day, twenty-five-year old English medical student, Roger Bannister decided to make an all-out effort to conquer the 4-minute mile barrier. As Bannister noted, "Whether we athletes liked it or not, the four-minute mile had become rather like [Mount] Everest—a challenge to the human spirit. It was a barrier that seemed to defy all attempts to break it—an awesome reminder that man's striving might be in vain."[53]

For several years beforehand, top milers such as Bannister, John Landy of Australia, and Wes Santee of the United States had been flirting with the mark, but none could break it. On the morning of May 6, Bannister nearly called off his latest attempt. Gusty winds made the odds of breaking the record even more formidable. But after much debate, Bannister decided to go for it.

Bannister's teammates on the British Amateur Athletic Club, Chris Brasher and Chris Chataway, agreed to set a brisk pace for Bannister. They got a little carried away, taking their teammate through the first quarter mile in a sizzling 57.5 seconds. By the third lap, all three runners had slowed down so much that a record appeared unlikely. At that point, Bannister reached down deep within himself for a strong finishing kick. Nearly numb with exhaustion, he ran his final lap in 58.9 seconds to break the tape at 3:59.4.

In proving that the 4-minute barrier was humanly possible, Bannister became the most famous miler of all time. Ironically, he never won a medal of any kind in the Olympics. He managed only a fourth-place finish in his sole Olympic race in 1952.

On May 6, 1954, English runner Roger Bannister became the first person to run the mile in less than four minutes.

Abebe Bikila

Spectators at the 1960 Olympics were puzzled by the unknown man who was keeping up with the leaders in the marathon while running barefoot through the streets of Rome. The barefoot runner was Abebe Bikila, the son of an Ethiopian shepherd and a member of the Ethiopian palace guard, who did not even own a pair of running shoes. Bikila stunned the experts by pulling away from favored Abdeslam Ben Rhadi of Morocco in the final mile to win the gold medal.

Four years later, Bikila's hopes of defending his marathon title were dealt a severe blow when he had to undergo an emergency operation to remove his appendix a month before the Olympics. But Bikila recovered quickly. Running in shoes this time, he breezed to an easy victory over a tough field of competitors. After beating the old Olympic record by eight minutes and finishing out of sight of his closest rival, Bikila then delighted the crowd by doing calisthenics on the infield grass, as fresh as if he had just run a morning jog.

Bikila's career ended in tragedy when he was paralyzed in an automobile accident in 1969. He died four years later at the age of forty-one.

Herb Elliot

Rival middle distance runners joked before the 1960 Olympics that the only way to beat Herb Elliot was to tie his legs together. No one ever found a legal alternative to that strategy. In forty-four races at 1,500 meters or its equivalent, the mile, Elliot never lost.

Elliot trained for his event on the sand dunes of Portsea, Australia, under the direction of coach Percy Cerutty. After surviving the incredibly brutal workouts devised by Cerutty, the actual races were a breeze for Elliot. He never bothered to study his opponents and often did not even know their names. At the Rome Olympics, he breezed along at a brisk pace for two and a half laps. With 600 yards to go, he took off on a long, hard finishing kick that demolished his opponents and broke his own world record with a time of 3:35.6.

Elliot's career was surprisingly brief. Having reached the top at age twenty-two, and no longer wanting to participate in torturous workouts, Elliot retired from competition after the 1960 Olympics.

Alberto Juantorena

At 6 feet, 2 inches, the long-legged Alberto Juantorena glided down the track with perhaps the longest strides in track and field history, earning himself the nickname "El Caballo," (The Horse). But what made him successful, according to U.S. rival Fred Newhouse was that "he had that ability to maintain his peak speed much longer than anyone else."[54]

Juantorena took up track and field late in life, switching over from basketball at the age of nineteen. He won every 400-meter race he ran during the 1973 and 1974 sea-

THE GREATEST UPSET

Discouraged with trying to uphold his dignity in the white man's world of sport, Billy Mills, an Oglala Sioux from the Pine Ridge Reservation in South Dakota quit running in 1962, but after joining the U.S. Marines, Mills decided to give it one more try. He had no illusions of winning an Olympic medal; his goal was simply to make the 1964 U.S. Olympic team, although even that seemed highly unlikely. At the trials, however, Mills ran the fastest race of his life to finish a distant second to Gerry Lindgren in the 10,000 meters to earn a spot on the U.S. team.

The idea of Mills winning a medal at the Olympics seemed unlikely. His best time at the distance was 29:10.4. World record holder Ron Clarke of Australia had run 28:15.6. Even if Mills ran the fastest 5,000 meters of his life and then kept going to run the next 5,000 meters even faster, he would still finish nearly a lap behind Clarke. Yet Mills knew he had a powerful finishing kick for a distance runner. He thought if he only could stay with Clarke, he could outsprint him to the tape.

During the race, Clarke maintained a murderous pace that wore down his major rivals. Running far faster than he ever had before at this distance, Mills struggled mightily to maintain contact. With about 1,000 meters to go, Clarke looked around and saw only Mills and Mohamed Gammoudi of Tunisia still with him. Neither were ranked among the world's better runners, and Clarke was convinced the race was his.

Both men, however, clung doggedly to

Billy Mills obliterates his own best time, setting an Olympic record in the 10,000-meter race.

Clarke's heels. The final lap degenerated into a wild scramble as the three men fought their way past runners who were a lap behind. Clarke and Gammoudi began to pull away from Mills.

Going into the final turn, Mills found, to his amazement, that he was still within striking distance. Coming wide off the turn, he shot past the stunned Clarke. Flying down the track with sprinter's speed, he ran down Gammoudi 30 yards from the finish and glided to the tape. In winning the gold, Mills clipped a mind-boggling 46 seconds off his previous best time to set an Olympic record of 28:24.4.

sons, only to be sidelined with two foot operations. Juantorena recovered in time to enter the 1976 Olympics. His coaches persuaded him to try running the 800 meters at those

Olympics, even though he had almost no experience in the event.

"El Caballo" put on an incredible display of speed and endurance during the 1976

Florence Griffith Joyner raises her arms in victory after winning the 100-meter dash at the 1988 Seoul Olympics.

Olympics. He trailed Fred Newhouse in the 400 meters, until the final straightaway. As he later explained, "I caught Newhouse in the last 50 meters because I have power and muscles I keep for the last part of the race."[55]

Juantorena's powerful finishing kick more than made up for his lack of experience in the 800 meters. Not only did he win the gold, but he crossed the finish line in a world record time of 1:43.5. In more than a century of Olympic competition, no other runner has ever won both the 400- and 800-meter races.

Florence Griffith Joyner

Flo Jo, as the Californian was nicknamed, took the track world by storm in 1988. After enjoying a decent but not spectacular career as a sprinter, she rededicated herself to the sport following her marriage to Al Joyner, the brother of heptathlon superstar Jackie Joyner. She also decided to use track as an outlet for creative expression. She began designing her own track uniforms with splashy colors, and painted her long fingernails before races to match her outfits.

THE GREATEST FEAT IN TRACK AND FIELD HISTORY

Bob Beamon, a twenty-one-year old native of New York, went into the 1968 Mexico City Olympic Games as a slight favorite in the long jump. During the year, he had won twenty-two of twenty-three competitions and had claimed the world indoor record with a jump of 27 feet, 1 inch. The only reason he was not favored more heavily was because he was prone to foul. Two other favored athletes, Ralph Boston of the United States and Lynn Davies of Great Britain, were less athletic but more technically sound jumpers than Beamon. Such jumpers often performed in high-pressure situations such as the Olympics. Beamon reinforced doubts about his performance by barely advancing to the finals.

The finals were held under heavy clouds with the constant threat of rain. Beamon, the fourth jumper out of seventeen finalists, stewed about his tendency to foul as he prepared for his turn. He took off down the runway, thinking of nothing more than getting a legal jump in to start the competition. Beamon hit the takeoff board perfectly. The gangly, 6-foot, 3-inch athlete soared high in the air. As he descended over the sand pit, he stretched his legs as far forward as they could go. Immediately, Beamon knew he had performed one of the best jumps of his career. But in his wildest dreams, he did not imagine the scope of what he had accomplished. He did not notice the stricken looks of his competitors who could not believe that a human could jump as far as Beamon just had.

Beamon's first clue that something special had happened came when the optical measuring device fell off the end of the rail. Beamon had gone beyond the farthest distance it could measure. A tape measure was produced, that put Beamon's distance at 8.9 meters.

Not being familiar with metric distances, Beamon still did not know why fans and competitors were buzzing. Finally, he learned that he had leaped 29 feet, 2 inches. He had not only topped the previous record, he had absolutely obliterated it. In the thirty three years since Jesse Owens's record jump, the world record had advanced a total of 8 1/2 inches. Beamon had soared 21 3/4 inches past the old record. Upon hearing this, Beamon's legs gave way and he sank to the ground in shock.

After only four jumps, the long jump competition was over. According to David Wallechinsky in *The Complete Book of the Olympics*, Lynn Davies turned to Ralph Boston and said, "I can't go on. What is the point? We'll all look silly." The others did complete their jumps but did so in a daze.

As for Beamon, he could not go on either. He retired shortly after the Olympics. After accomplishing what many track and field experts described as the greatest feat in the 3,000-year history of the sport, a feat that he could never duplicate, he had nothing else to shoot for.

Bob Beamon soars a remarkable 29 feet, 2 inches in the long jump, an Olympic record that still stands.

Wearing her most flamboyant suits, including a hooded one that eventually was adopted by runners throughout the world, Flo Jo flew down the track at the 1988 U.S. Olympic Trials in a world record 10.49 seconds. Her time broke the old mark by .27 seconds, an incredible margin for such a short race.

At the 1988 Seoul Olympics, Flo Jo ran away from the field in the 100 meters. She then left the world with a timeless image of grace and speed in the 200 meters. Sensing what she accomplished as she blazed out of the turn, Flo Jo said that she, "felt so happy inside I just had to let it out."[56] As she effortlessly breezed to the finish line, her smile widened and she raised her arms in pure joy as she hit the tape in a world record time of 21.34 seconds in the 200 meters. Griffith Joyner completed her career by anchoring the U.S. team to victory in the 4 x 100 meter relay. She retired owning the fastest seven times ever run by a woman at 100 meters.

Michael Johnson

No one could mistake Michael Johnson running in a meet. Even if he were not always in the lead, even if he were not wearing his gaudy gold shoes, he would have been distinguished by his unique, straight-up sprinting style. That style led the twenty-eight-year old Texan to dominate the 200- and 400-meter sprints.

As the 1996 Atlanta Olympics approached, there was no doubt as to who the star of the track and field events would be. Rival sprinter Ato Bolden of Trinidad and Tobago had to admit that he and the others were running for second place. "[Michael's only] vulnerable if he loses a shoe,"[57] cracked Bolden.

At Atlanta, Johnson became the first man in history to win both the 200- and 400-meter sprints. His 200-meter performance was breathtaking. Johnson shot out of the starting blocks and roared off the curve far ahead of his rivals. Running effortlessly, he toured the final 100 meters in 9.2 seconds, faster than any human has ever run before. His time of 19.32 seconds annihilated his own previous mark of 19.66. Four years later, Johnson solidified his place in history by becoming the first man to successfully defend his Olympic 400-meter title.

Carl Lewis

Carl Lewis grew up in the world of track and field, the son of two track coaches. When they started their own track club, seven-year old Carl spent his time building castles in the long jump pit. Eventually, Carl began competing, and began building his own dreams out of that same long jump pit. The speed that gave him the momentum to soar far into the sand pit also carried him to fame in the sprints. By 1981, Lewis ranked first in the world in both the 100 meters and the long jump. Three years later, he was ready to go after his most ambitious dream—matching the Olympic performance of the legendary Jesse Owens, star of the 1936 Berlin games.

Carl Lewis (left) receives a silver medal in the 100-meter sprint; he was later awarded the gold medal when winner Ben Johnson tested positive for steroids.

At the 1984 Games, Lewis stood up to the crushing media pressure that accompanied his quest. In the 100 meters, he overcame a shaky start to pull even with the leaders at 80 meters. He finished the final 20 meters so strongly that he won the event by a good 8 feet, the largest winning margin in Olympic history. Lewis then cruised to equally convincing victories in his other events, the 200 meters, long jump, and 4 x 100 relay, thereby matching Owens's accomplishment.

Whereas Owens was a strict amateur who never reaped financial rewards from his efforts, Lewis lived in a time of affluence for track athletes. Earning a fortune just for appearing at meets and for endorsing products, he was able to enjoy a long track and field career. In 1988, he earned a controversial second gold medal in the 100 meters after the winner, Canada's Ben Johnson, was disqualified for steroid use. Then Lewis captured his second long jump title with a breathtaking leap of 28 feet, 7 inches in the same Olympics. Although age forced him to give way to younger rivals in the sprint events, he captured yet another long jump gold medal in 1992.

disappointment. At that point, the veteran Olympian took a moment to calm himself with words that would have made Baron de Coubertin proud. "I had to get back to what I had told myself months before: don't try to win the Olympics. Just compete well."[58] The change in philosophy relaxed Lewis. Not only did he compete well, he sailed to his fourth consecutive gold medal in the long jump, closing out his Olympic career with nine gold medals.

Bob Matthias

For most athletes, an Olympic gold medal is the end result of many years of hard work and sacrifice. Bob Matthias, however, stumbled on his first gold medal by accident in 1948. During the spring of his senior year at Tulare High School in California, Matthias was approached by his track coach with a proposition. "I've just heard about some event called the decathlon that will be included in a meet in Los Angeles about a week after you graduate," the coach said. "It will give you something to do after you get out of school."[59]

Bob Matthias, the only two-time Olympic decathlon champion.

At the age of thirty-five, long past his prime, Lewis decided to give the Olympics one last try. He struggled at the U.S. trials and managed to capture the third and final spot on the U.S. team in the long jump by a margin of one inch. Then, at the 1996 Atlanta Games, he performed poorly and looked as if he would finish his career in

Without even knowing what a decathlon was, Matthias agreed to enter. Not only did he win, but he made the U.S. Olympic team. At the London Olympic Games, Matthias performed particularly well in the discus, javelin, high jump, and pole vault despite miserable, rainy conditions. The decathlon ran so long that officials had to drive cars into the stadium and turn on the lights so the athletes could see. At 10:35 P.M. that night, an exhausted, seventeen-year old Matthias stunned the world by winning the decathlon.

After winning the event on raw talent in 1948, a fully prepared, well-trained Matthias was a virtual shoo-in to capture the gold four years later. He did not disappoint, beating his 1948 marks in almost every event to become the only person to repeat as Olympic decathlon champion.

THE STREAK

Once a world class hurdler gets his rhythm down, he can be almost impossible to beat. U.S. 110-meter hurdler Harrison Dillard won eighty two consecutive races in the 1940s and 1950s. But even that mark fell far short of the unbeaten streak of 400-meter hurdler Edwin Moses.

In an era when most top athletes received expert coaching, Moses was a self-made hurdler. The Ohio native attended Morehouse College in Atlanta to get an engineering degree. Despite the fact that Morehouse did not have a track, Moses took up running the 400-meter hurdles at a neighborhood track and showed exceptional talent. Moses was the only hurdler in the world capable of running with such long strides that he required only thirteen strides between each hurdle.

Moses had never even competed internationally before running in his first Olympics in 1976. He showed no jitters, winning the gold medal in his event at the 1976 Olympics in a world record time of 47.63. He had not even begun to hit his peak, however. The streak that was to make him famous began on September 2, 1977, when he won a competition in Germany. Although forced to miss the 1980 Olympics due to the U.S. boycott, Moses never let up on his training. He came back to win gold at the 1984 Olympics, as well as every contest in between.

As his streak approached 100 races, people began to wonder if Moses would ever lose. On June 4, 1987, Moses finally proved that he could be beaten. On that day, Iowa State University hurdler Danny Harris, who was eleven years younger than Moses, clipped the veteran at the finish line by .13 seconds. Moses's streak finally ended at 102 consecutive victories.

For almost a decade, hurdler Edwin Moses won every event he competed in.

Al Oerter

Few athletes have shown the grit and toughness of Al Oerter, a discus thrower from West Babylon, New York. In the 1956 Olympics, the twenty-year old uncorked the best throw of his career up to that point to upset the favorites and claim the gold medal in his event. He recovered from a near-fatal traffic accident the following year and still made the U.S. Olympic team in 1960. There he lagged behind his giant teammate, Rink Babka until late in the competition when he came through with another clutch effort. His winning toss of 194 feet, 2 inches sailed 10 feet further than his previous Olympic effort. Two years later, Oerter became the first person to hurl the discus more than 200 feet.

Oerter should not have attempted his third Olympics, the 1964 Tokyo Games. He suffered from a neck injury and torn cartilage in his lower ribs, either of which should have kept him on the sidelines. Even after taking a shot of novocaine to numb the pain, wrapping his ribs in tape, and putting on a neck harness, Oerter could hardly throw. "I was thinking of dropping out," Oerter admitted. "Then the competition came and the adrenaline started flowing and everything worked."[60] Somehow, Oerter managed a throw of 200 feet, 1½ inches, to win gold medal number three.

Even a healthy Oerter appeared to have no chance to win when he entered the 1968 Olympics in Mexico City. The best throw of his career lagged 17 feet behind the world record of his U.S. teammate, Jay Silvester. Oerter, however, was the ultimate competitor. While his competitors struggled in the Olympic spotlight, Oerter hurled what was by far the best throw of his life. His Olympic record toss of 212 feet, 6½ inches earned him his fourth consecutive gold medal, a feat all the more astounding in that at least three of his four victories were major upsets.

Emil Zatopek

Watching Czechoslovakian distance runner Emil Zatopek run was like watching a criminal being flogged with a whip. He gasped and wheezed and moaned and lurched in such apparent agony that his finishes were often painful to watch. Looks were deceiving, however. Zatopek could outlast any runner of his time over any distance 5,000 meters or longer. He set eighteen world records during his six-year dominance of world distance running from 1948 to 1954. During that time, he won thirty eight straight races at his favorite distance, 10,000 meters. Like Herb Elliot, Zatopek's success was a result of his almost superhuman ability to withstand the most agonizing workouts. Running in heavy army boots, he would run lap after lap of the track until he could barely stand.

Despite his fanatical competitiveness, Zatopek was one of the most popular and outgoing distance runners in history. Fluent in several languages, he enjoyed talking to both competitors and spectators as he ran. During one preliminary Olympic

Czech runner Emil Zatopek crosses the finish line in record time to win the 10,000 meters at the 1948 London Olympics.

race, when it was obvious which runners would qualify, Zatopek stepped aside and directed the other runners to the finish like a traffic cop.

Zatopek completely wore down his opposition in the 10,000 meters in the 1948 Games in London. He lapped all but two runners and finished nearly 300 meters ahead of the silver medalist. His greatest triumph, though, came at the 1952 Olympics in

Helsinki, Finland. Zatopek grunted and flailed his way to narrower victories in both the 5,000 meters and 10,000 meters. He then entered the marathon, a race he had never run before. For most of the race, he ran with Jim Peters of Great Britain, one of the favorites in the race.

At one point, Zatopek questioned Peters about the pace. "Jim, the pace—it is too fast?"[61] he asked. Peters had actually

95

been forcing the pace as much as he dared in an effort to wear out Zatopek, who had already run tough races at the other distances. Hoping to discourage Zatopek, he told him the pace was actually too slow. Zatopek merely shrugged and sped up, leaving Peters and the others behind. Zatopek chatted with police escorts and spectators until he reached the finish line far ahead of his opposition. The win made him the first person to win the 5,000 meters, 10,000 meters, and the marathon. Given the fact that the increased size of the Olympics has forced officials to add several preliminary heats of both the 5,000 and 10,000, it is unlikely any runner would have the stamina to get through all the races necessary to duplicate his feat.

Awards and Statistics

Track and Field Olympic Records

Men's Records

Event	Record	Athlete	Nation	Host Location	Date
100 m	9.84	Donovan Bailey	CAN	Atlanta	July 27, '96
200 m	19.32	Michael Johnson	USA	Atlanta	Aug. 01, '96
400 m	43.49	Michael Johnson	USA	Atlanta	July 29, '96
800 m	1:42.58	Vebjorn Rodahl	NOR	Atlanta	July 31, '96
1,500 m	3:32.07	Noah Kiprono Ngenyi	KEN	Sydney	Sept. 29, '00
5,000 m	13:05.59	Said Aouita	MOR	Los Angeles	Aug. 11, '84
10,000 m	27:07.34	Haile Gebrselassie	ETH	Atlanta	July 29, '96
marathon	2:09:21	Carlos Lopes	POR	Los Angeles	Aug. 12, '84
3,000 m steeplechase	8:05.51	Julius Kariuki	KEN	Seoul	Sept. 30, '88
110 m hurdles	12.95	Allen Johnson	USA	Atlanta	July 29, '96
400 m hurdles	46.78	Kevin Young	USA	Barcelona	Aug. 06, '92
high jump	2.39 m	Charles Austin	USA	Atlanta	July 28, '96
pole vault	5.92 m	Jean Galfione	FRA	Atlanta	Aug. 02, '96
		Igor Trandenkov	RUS	Atlanta	Aug. 02, '96
		Andrei Timonchik	GER	Atlanta	Aug. 02, '96
long jump	8.90 m	Bob Beamon	USA	Mexico	Oct. 18, '68
triple jump	18.09 m	Kenny Harrison	USA	Atlanta	July 27, '96
shot put	22.47 m	Ulf Timmermann	E. GER	Seoul	Sept. 23, '88
discus	69.40 m	Lars Riedel	GER	Atlanta	July 31, '96
hammer throw	84.80 m	Sergey Litvinov	USR	Seoul	Sept. 26, '88
javelin	89.66 m	Jan Zelezny	CZE	Barcelona	Aug. 08, '92
decathlon	8,847 points	Daley Thompson	GBR	Los Angeles	Aug. 08/09, '96
20 km walk	1:18:59	Robert Korzeniowski	POL	Sydney	Sept. 22, '00
50 km walk	3:38:29	Vyacheslav Ivanenko	USSR	Seoul	Sept. 30, '88
4 x 100 m	37.40	Mike Marsh	USA	Barcelona	Aug. 08, '92
		Leroy Burrell			
		Dennis Mitchell			
		Carl Lewis			
4 x 400 m	2:55.74	Andrew Valmon	USA	Barcelona	Aug. 08, '92
		Quincy Watts			
		Michael Johnson			
		Steve Lewis			

Women's Records

Event	Record	Athlete	Nation	Host Location	Date
100 m	10.62	Florence Griffith Joyner	USA	Seoul	Sept. 24, '88
200 m	21.34	Florence Griffith Joyner	USA	Seoul	Sept. 29, '88
400 m	48.25	Marie-Jose Perec	FRA	Atlanta	July 29, '96
800 m	1:53.43	Nadezhda Olizarenko	USSR	Moscow	July 27, '80
1,500 m	3:53.96	Paula Ivan	ROM	Seoul	Oct. 01, '88
5,000 m	14:40.79	Gabriela Szabo	ROM	Sydney	Sept. 25, '00
10,000 m	30:17.49	Derartu Tulu	ETH	Sydney	Sept. 30, '00
marathon	2:23.14	Naono Takahashi	JAP	Sydney	Sept. 24, '00
100 m hurdles	12.38	Yordanka Donkova	BUL	Seoul	Sept. 30, '88
400 m hurdles	52.82	Dione Hemmings	JAM	Atlanta	July 31, '96
high jump	2.05 m	Stefka Kostadinova	BUL	Atlanta	Aug. 03, '96
pole vault	4.60m	Stacy Dragila	USA	Sydney	Sept. 27, '00
long jump	7.40 m	Jackie Joyner-Kersee	USA	Seoul	Sept. 29, '88
triple jump	15.33 m	Inessa Kravets	UKR	Atlanta	July 31, '96
shot put	22.41 m	Ilona Slupianek	E. GER	Moscow	July 24, '80
discus	72.30 m	Martina Hellmann	E. GER	Seoul	Sept. 29, '88
hammer throw	71.16 m	Kamila Skolimowska	POL	Sydney	Sept. 29, '00
javelin	74.68 m	Petra Felke	E. GER	Seoul	Sept. 26, '88
heptathlon	7,291 points	Jackie Joyner-Kersee	USA	Seoul	Sept. 23/24, '88
10 km walk	44.32	Yueling Chen	CHN	Barcelona	Aug. 03, '92
20 km walk	1:29.05	Wang Liping	CHN	Sydney	Sept. 27, '00
4 x 100 m	41.60	Romy Müller Bärbel Wöckel Ingrid Auerswald Marlies Göhr	E. GER	Moscow	Aug. 01, '80
4 x 400 m	3:15.17	Tatiana Ledovskaya Olga Nazarova Maria Pinigina Olga Bryzgina	USSR	Seoul	Aug. 01, '88

Track and Field World Records

Event	Time/Distance	Type	Athlete	Nation	Date
100 m	9.79	Men	Maurice Greene	USA	June 16, '99
100 m	10.49	Women	Florence Griffith Joyner	USA	July 16, '88
200 m	19.32	Men	Michael Johnson	USA	Aug. 01, '96
200 m	21.34	Women	Florence Griffith Joyner	USA	Sept. 29, '88
400 m	43.18	Men	Michael Johnson	USA	Aug. 26, '99
400 m	47.60	Women	Marita Koch	E. GER	Oct. 10, '85
800 m	1:41.11	Men	Wilson Kipketer	DEN	Aug. 24, '97
800 m	1:53.28	Women	Jarmila Kratochvilova	CZE	July 07, '83
1,500 m	3:26.00	Men	Hitcham El Guerrouj	MOR	July 14, '98
1,500 m	3:50.46	Women	Qu Yunxia	CHN	Sept. 11, '93
3,000 m	7:20.67	Men	Daniel Komen	KEN	Sept. 01, '96
5,000 m	12:39.36	Men	Haile Gebrselassie	ETH	June 13, '98
5,000 m	14:28.09	Women	Jiang Bo	CHN	Oct. 23, '97
10,000 m	26:22.75	Men	Haile Gebrselassie	ETH	June 01, '98

Event	Time/Distance	Type	Athlete	Nation	Date
10,000 m	29:31.78	Women	Junxia Wang	CHN	Sept. 08, '93
marathon	2:05:42	Men	Khalid Khannouchi	MOR	Oct. 24, '99
marathon	2:20:43	Women	Tegla Loroupe	KEN	Sept. 29, '99
3000 m steeplechase	7:55:72	Men	Bernard Barmasai	KEN	Aug. 24, '97
110 m hurdles	12.91	Men	Colin Jackson	GBR	Aug. 20, '93
100 m hurdles	12.21	Women	Yordanka Donkova	BUL	Aug. 08, '88
400 m hurdles	46.78	Men	Kevin Young	USA	Aug. 06, '92
400 m hurdles	52.61	Women	Kim Batten	USA	Aug. 11, '95
high jump	2.45 m	Men	Javier Sotomayor	CUB	July 27, '93
high jump	2.09 m	Women	Stefka Kostadinova	BUL	Aug. 30, '87
pole vault	6.14 m	Men	Sergei Bubka	UKR	July 31, '94
pole vault	4.63* m	Women	Stacy Dragila	USA	July 23, '00
long jump	8.95 m	Men	Mike Powell	USA	Aug. 08, '91
long jump	7.52 m	Women	Galina Chistyakova	RUS	June 11, '88
triple jump	18.29 m	Men	Jonathan Edwards	GBR	Aug. 07, '95
triple jump	15.50 m	Women	Inessa Kravets	UKR	Aug. 10, '95
shot put	23.12 m	Men	Randy Barnes	USA	May 20, '90
shot put	22.63 m	Women	Natalya Lisovskaya	USSR	June 07, '87
discus	74.08 m	Men	Jurgen Schutt	E. GER	June 06, '86
discus	76.80 m	Women	Gabriele Reinsch	E. GER	July 09, '88
hammer throw	86.74 m	Men	Yuriy Sedykh	USSR	Aug. 30, '86
javelin	98.48 m	Men	Jan Zelezny	CZE	May 25, '96
javelin	69.48 m	Women	Trine Hattestad	NOR	July 28, '00
decathlon	8,994 points	Men	Tomas Dvorak	CZE	July 04, '99
heptathlon	7,291 points	Women	Jackie Joyner-Kersee	USA	Sept. 24, '88
20 km walk	1:17:25.6	Men	Bernard Segura	MEX	May 07, '94
20 km walk	1:37:19.1	Women	Ailing Xue	CHN	Sept. 18, '99
50 km walk	3:40:57.9	Men	Thierry Toutain	FRA	Sept. 29, '96
4x100 m	37.40	Men	USA	USA	Aug. 08, '92
					Aug. 21, '93
4 x 100 m	41.37	Women	GDR	E. GER	Oct. 06, '85
4 x 400 m	2:54.20	Men	USA	USA	July 22, '98
4 x 400 m	3:15.17	Women	USSR	USSR	Oct. 01, '88

* Awaiting Ratification

Notes

Introduction:
The Purest of Sport

1. Quoted in Lewis H. Carlson and John J. Fogarty, *Tales of Gold*. Chicago: Contemporary, 1987, p. 365.

Chapter 1: The Olympics:
Birth and Rebirth of
Track and Field

2. Ralph Hickock, *New Encyclopedia of Sports*. New York: McGraw-Hill, 1977, p. 469.
3. Tom McNab, *The Complete Book of Track and Field*. New York: Exeter Books, 1980, p. 102.
4. John Cumming, *Runners and Walkers*. Chicago: Regnery Gateway, 1981, p. 129.
5. Quoted in John A. Lucas, *The Future of the Olympic Games*. Champaign, IL: Human Kinetics, 1992, p. 92.
6. Carlson and Fogarty, *Tales of Gold*, p. 29.
7. Quoted in Carlson and Fogarty, *Tales of Gold*, p. 49.
8. McNab, *The Complete Book of Track and Field*, p. 15.

Chapter 2: Evolution of
Track and Field

9. Quoted in *Track & Field: The New York Times Encyclopedia of Sports, Vol. 4*. New York: Arno, 1979, p. 16.
10. Quoted in *Track & Field: The New York Times Encyclopedia of Sports, Vol. 4*, p. 16.
11. Quoted in Carlson and Fogarty, *Tales of Gold*, p. 244.

Chapter 3: Breaking the
Gender Barrier

12. Quoted in Caroline Searle and Bryn Vaile, eds., *Official Olympic Companion*. London: Brassy's Sports, 1996, p. 2.
13. Quoted in Allen Guttman, *Women's Sports: A History*. New York: Columbia University Press, 1991, p. 34.
14. Janet Wollum, *Outstanding Women Athletes*. Phoenix: Oryx, 1992, p. ix.
15. Quoted in Guttman, *Women's Sports: A History*, p. 163.
16. Quoted in Guttman, *Women's Sports: A History*, p. 188.
17. Quoted in Louise Mead Tricard, *American Women's Track & Field*.

Jefferson, North Carolina: McFarland, 1996, p. 176.

18. Quoted in Guttman, *Women's Sports: A History*, p. 140.

19. Quoted in Carlson and Fogarty, *Tales of Gold*, p. 58.

20. Quoted in *Track & Field: The New York Times Encyclopedia of Sports, Vol. 4*, p. 13.

21. Quoted in Tricard, *American Women's Track & Field*, p. 403.

22. Quoted in David Wallechinsky, *The Complete Book of the Olympics*. Boston: Little, Brown, 1991, p. 207.

23. Quoted in Alexandra Wolff, "Time Capsule," *Sports Illustrated*, October 18, 2000, p. 63.

Chapter 4: The Political Burden of Track and Field

24. Quoted in Susan D. Bachrach, *The Nazi Olympics*. Boston: Little, Brown, 2000, p. 82.

25. Quoted in Bachrach, *The Nazi Olympics*, p. 49.

26. Wallechinsky, *The Complete Book of the Olympics*, p. 9.

27. Quoted in Doug Gilbert, *The Miracle Machine*. New York: Coward, McCann and Geoghegan, 1980, p. 213.

28. McNab, *The Complete Book of Track and Field*, p. 16.

29. Quoted in Baruch Hazan, *Olympic Sports and Propaganda Games, Moscow 1980*. New Brunswick, NJ: Transaction Books, 1982, p. 36.

30. Quoted in Yuri Brolchin, *The Big Red Machine*. New York: Random House, 1978, p. 7.

31. Quoted in Gilbert, *The Miracle Machine*, p. 9.

32. Quoted in Carlson and Fogarty, *Tales of Gold*, p. 179.

33. Quoted in Al Silverman, ed., *The Best of Sport*. New York: Viking, 1971, p. 442.

34. Quoted in Wallechinsky, *The Complete Book of the Olympics*, p. 22.

35. Quoted in Wallechinsky, *The Complete Book of the Olympics*, p. 22.

36. Wallechinsky, *The Complete Book of the Olympics*, p. 22.

37. Quoted in Robert Sullivan, "Field of Dreams," *Time*, October 9, 2000, p. 98.

Chapter 5: Cheating: The Bane of Track and Field

38. Cumming, *Runners and Walkers*, p. 150.

39. Quoted in Cumming, *Runners and Walkers*, p. 134.

40. Lucas, *The Future of the Olympic Games*, p. 123.

41. Quoted in *Track & Field: The New York Times Encyclopedia of Sports, Vol. 4*, p. 2.

42. Quoted in Arch Ward, ed., *The Greatest Sports Stories from the Chicago Tribune*. New York: A. S. Barnes, 1953, p. 202.

43. Quoted in Ward, *The Greatest Sports Stories from the Chicago Tribune*, p. 296.

44. Quoted in *Track & Field, The New York Times Encyclopedia of Sports, Vol. 4*, p. 72.

45. Quoted in *Track & Field, The New York Times Encyclopedia of Sports, Vol. 4*, p. vii.

46. Quoted in Brolchin, *The Big Red Machine*, p. 126.

47. Quoted in Gilbert, *The Miracle Machine*, p. 201.

48. Quoted in Gilbert, *The Miracle Machine*, p. 200.

49. Quoted in Lucas, *The Future of the Olympic Games*, p. 105.

50. Quoted in Lucas, *The Future of the Olympic Games*, p. 108.

51. Quoted in Douglas Collins, *Olympic Dreams*. New York: Universe Press, 1996, p. 221.

52. Quoted in Gilbert, *The Miracle Machine*, p. 201.

Chapter 6: Stars of Track and Field

53. Quoted in Eric Olson, *On the Right Track*. Indianapolis: Bobbs-Merrill, 1984, p. 81.

54. Quoted in Carlson and Fogarty, *Tales of Gold*, p. 479.

55. Quoted in *Track & Field, The New York Times Encyclopedia of Sports, Vol. 4*, p. 193.

56. Quoted in Nathan Aaseng, *Florence Griffith Joyner: Dazzling Olympian*. Minneapolis: Lerner Publications, 1989.

57. Quoted in Mark Starr, "Gone With the Wind," *Newsweek*, August 12, 1996, p. 21.

58. Quoted in Frank DeFord, "Touching Down," *Newsweek*, August 12, 1996, p. 28.

59. Quoted in Carlson and Fogarty, *Tales of Gold*, p. 204.

60. Quoted in *Track & Field, The New York Times Encyclopedia of Sports, Vol. 4*, p. 155.

61. Quoted in Wallechinsky, *The Complete Book of the Olympics*, p. 58.

For Further Reading

Nathan Aaseng, *American Indian Lives: Athletes*. New York: Facts On File, 1996. Biographies of Native American athletes including track and field stars Jim Thorpe and Billy Mills.

——, *Florence Griffith Joyner: Dazzling Olympian*. Minneapolis: Lerner Publications, 1989. Chronicles the emergence of the sprinter during the 1988 Olympics as the world's fastest woman.

——, *Women Olympic Champions*. San Diego: Lucent, 2000. More in-depth coverage of track stars Didriksen, Blankers-Koen, and Joyner-Kersee.

Dave Anderson, *Story of the Olympics*. New York: William Morrow, 1996. Brief, readable episodes of Olympic lore.

Bud Greenspan, *100 Greatest Moments in Olympic History*. Los Angeles: General Publishing, 1995. Capsule descriptions of the most outstanding performances in the Olympics.

Jackie Joyner-Kersee with Sonja Steptoe, *A Kind of Grace*. New York: Warner, 1997. Interesting, first-person account of the athlete's difficult childhood and Olympic challenges.

Carl Lewis, *Inside Track*. New York: Simon and Schuster, 1992. One of the all-time greats tells what the world of track and field was like during the transition time from amateur to professional sports.

Sally Point, *Finding Their Stride: A Team of Young Runners and Their Season of Triumph*. San Diego: Harcourt, 2000. Upbeat story of a high school track team in Bethlehem, Pennsylvania.

Works Consulted

Books

Susan D. Bachrach, *The Nazi Olympics*. Boston: Little, Brown, 2000. Chilling and detailed account of the political maneuverings of the 1936 Olympics.

Yuri Brolchin, *The Big Red Machine*. New York: Random House, 1978. A behind-the-scenes look at the often mysterious world of Soviet athletes during the Cold War.

Lewis H. Carlson and John J. Fogarty, *Tales of Gold*. Chicago: Contemporary, 1987. First-person accounts by Olympic participants of their experiences.

Douglas Collins, *Olympic Dreams*. New York: Universe Press, 1996. Takes a more personal view than some histories of the athletes' quest for gold.

John Cumming, *Runners and Walkers*. Chicago: Regnery Gateway, 1981. Brings to light little-known stories of nineteenth century track and field champions.

Doug Gilbert, *The Miracle Machine*. New York: Coward, McCann and Geoghegan, 1980. Fairly sympathetic treatment of the East German focus on sports excellence in the 1970s.

Allen Guttman, *The Olympics*. Urbana: University of Illinois, 1992. Survey of major events in Olympic history.

————, *Women's Sports: A History*. New York: Columbia University Press, 1991. Thorough and readable account of the advances of women's sport in the twentieth century.

Baruch Hazan, *Olympic Sports and Propaganda Games, Moscow 1980*. New Brunswick, NJ: Transaction Books, 1982. A look at the political infighting that has frequently characterized the Olympics, particularly track and field.

Bill Henry, *An Approved History of the Olympic Games*. Los Angeles: Alfred Publishing Company, 1984. Another chronological overview of the Olympics.

Ralph Hickock, *New Encyclopedia of Sports*. New York: McGraw-Hill, 1977. An exhaustive, although somewhat outdated, chronicle of the sports world; the sections on track origins are insightful.

John A. Lucas, *The Future of the Olympic Games*. Champaign, IL: Human Kinetics, 1992. Delves more deeply than other books into the social context of the Olympics.

Tom McNab, *The Complete Book of Track and Field*. New York: Exeter Books, 1980. Lives up to its title as a thorough treatment of track and field history.

Eric Olson, *On the Right Track*. Indianapolis: Bobbs-Merrill, 1984. This collection of track and field stories includes some personal perspectives from the participants.

Caroline Searle and Bryn Vaile, eds., *Official Olympic Companion*. London: Brassy's Sports, 1996. Another almanac that also includes brief vignettes of select athletes.

Al Silverman, ed., *The Best of Sport*. New York: Viking, 1971. A compilation of sports stories over several decades from *Sport* magazine writers.

Track & Field: The New York Times Encyclopedia of Sports, Vol. 4. New York: Arno, 1979. Compilation of actual *New York Times* reports from the major events in the history of track and field.

Louise Mead Tricard, *American Women's Track & Field*. Jefferson, North Carolina: McFarland, 1996. Thorough history of women in the running, throwing, and jumping competitions.

David Wallechinsky, *The Complete Book of the Olympics*. Boston: Little, Brown, 1991. The most authoritative listing of Olympic winners, this book is also crammed with brief stories about the competition and/or the athletes who participated.

Arch Ward, ed., *The Greatest Sports Stories from the Chicago Tribune*. New York: A. S. Barnes, 1953. Sportswriting from the first half of the century.

Janet Wollum, *Outstanding Women Athletes*. Phoenix: Oryx, 1992. Straightforward accounts of star athletes.

Periodicals

Frank DeFord, "Touching Down," *Newsweek*, August 12, 1996.

Mark Starr, "Give Me Five," *Newsweek*, September 11, 2000.

————, "Gone With the Wind," *Newsweek*, August 12, 1996.

Robert Sullivan, "Field of Dreams," *Time*, October 9, 2000.

Alexandra Wolff, "Time Capsule," *Sports Illustrated*, October 18, 2000.

Index

Picture Credits

About the Author

Nathan Aaseng is the author of more than 150 books for young readers on a wide variety of subjects. Aaseng, from Eau Claire, Wisconsin, was a 1999 recipient of the Wisconsin Library Association's Notable Wisconsin Author award.